Understanding
the
Trauma
of
Childhood
Psycho-Sexual
Abuse

Elizabeth Adams

Mills & Sanderson, Publishers
Bedford, Massachusetts * 1994

Published by Mills & Sanderson, Publishers
41 North Road, Suite 201 • Bedford, MA 01730-1021
Copyright © 1994 Elizabeth Adams

If additional copies of this book are not available at your local bookstore, you may order direct from the publisher by calling **1-800-441-6224**. MasterCard and Visa welcome.

Library of Congress Cataloging-in-Publication Data

Adams, Elizabeth
      Understanding the trauma of childhood psycho-sexual abuse / Elizabeth Adams.
          p.   cm.
      Includes bibliographical references and index.
      ISBN 0-938179-38-1 :
          1. Adult child sexual abuse victims--United States--Psychology.
2. Adult child sexual abuse victims--Rehabilitation--United States.
I. Title.
HV6570.2.C36   1994
362.7'64'0973--dc20   94-1622
                                        CIP

Material credited to authors Carol Poston and Karen Lison originally appeared in *Reclaiming Our Lives: Hope for Adult Survivors of Incest*, copyright 1989, and is reprinted here by permission of Little, Brown and Company. Referenced material appears in a reprint edition released through Bantam Books/Bantam Doubleday Dell Publishing Group, Inc. in 1990.

Material credited to author Terrence Des Pres originally appeared in *The Survivor: An Anatomy of Life in the Death Camps*, copyright 1976, and is reprinted here by permission of Oxford University Press, Inc.

Printed and manufactured by Capital City Press.
Cover design by Lyrl Ahern.

Printed and Bound in the United States of America

To the millions of men and women who were abused when they were children, with the hope that they can find the strength to attempt the journey toward recovery; to the partners who are sharing survivors' lives and the professionals who are dedicating their lives to helping survivors heal, with heartfelt thanks; and to today's and tomorrow's children, with a prayer that they will never know the tragedy of childhood sexual abuse.

To my husband Walter, who knew something was wrong even before I did. His acceptance and willingness to stand beside me helped me find the strength to accept myself and the courage to heal.

Acknowledgments

I would like to acknowledge and thank some very special people who have played important roles in my healing process or the publication of this book.

Through previous writing collaborations, Nancy Schluntz helped me hone my editing skills, enabling me to grow confident in using the tool I chose for healing. Anne Donoghue, Susan Haynes, and Patricia Kelly helped me find the courage to face myself. Virginia Palmer has been my professional mentor and friend for over 20 years; she has often provided the light at the end of a dark tunnel by just listening.

There is no way I can adequately express my appreciation to the women who formed a protective circle around me when I was extremely vulnerable. Wendy Overin and Leslie Freerks provided the reality check that is so important to survivors. Laura Frings, Georgia Lang, and Linda Lynn formed my "group" of caring women. Dr. Gloria Enguidanos taught me how to take care of and love myself.

Margot Silk Forrest, editor of *The Healing Woman*, a monthly newsletter for women survivors of childhood sexual abuse, counseled on how to proceed with writing about my abuse experiences; through publishing some of my articles, she rejuvenated my belief in myself. She also granted permission for me to reprint material from several issues of her newsletter in this book.

Gloria Enguidanos, Ph.D., psychologist and professor; Bobbi Hoover, M.A., Licensed Marriage, Family, Child Counselor (MFCC); Cathy N. Peters, survivor; Carol Poston, survivor and author; Diana L. Smith, M.A. and lecturer graciously agreed to review my developing manuscript. I especially appreciate their efforts because I know how busy they are, and their input was invaluable!

John Briere, Associate Professor of Psychiatry at the University of Southern California School of Medicine; and Judith Lewis Herman, M.D., Associate Clinical Professor of Psychiatry at Harvard Medical

School, and Director of Training at the Victims of Violence Program in the Department of Psychiatry at Cambridge Hospital, Cambridge, Massachusetts kindly granted permission for me to reprint material contained in position papers presented at the 1993 Annual Meeting of the American Psychiatric Association.

Kathy Duguid, M.A., Licensed Marriage, Family, Child Counselor (MFCC); Vincent J. Felitti, M.D., head of the Department of Preventive Medicine at Kaiser Permanente in San Diego, California; Bobbi Hoover, a therapist listed previously with the manuscript reviewers; and Linda Meyer Williams, Ph.D., a Research Associate Professor at the University of New Hampshire Family Research Laboratory, a Senior Research Associate at Joseph J. Peters Institute in Philadelphia, and a member of the Executive Committee of the American Professional Society on the Abuse of Children (APSAC) graciously participated in telephone interviews and/or granted permission for information from their journal articles to be reprinted in this book.

In addition, Margaret Matthews (a pen name) and Barrie Ann Mason, both sexual abuse survivors, granted permission for material from articles they wrote based on their own experiences to be reprinted in this book.

Beverley Spencer granted permission for her dramatic drawings, which so graphically tell the story of the torment and healing she experienced, to be reprinted in this book.

I would also like to thank the people at Mills & Sanderson, Publishers for recognizing the importance of this book, especially publisher Jan H. Anthony for understanding my vision and helping to capture my dream.

Catherine Needham, Julie Robbins, and Valerie Scalera recently became a part of my world. Their sharing and validation provide a support system that I will carry with me into the future.

Finally, I extend my heartfelt appreciation to my family, especially to my husband. The tormented, fragmented world that encompasses survivors can't help but touch the lives of those they love. Although much of the person I have been was a mystery to my family, they never stopped loving me. Their love bolstered me as I searched for the strength to attempt recovery.

Contents

Popular Misconceptions About Childhood Sexual Abuse

#1: Perpetrators can be easily spotted.

#2: It is impossible for survivors of childhood sexual abuse to recover from the trauma of their past.

#3: The child could have prevented the assault.

#4: Survivors can't really block from their memory what happened to them in childhood.

#5: If the returning memories are real, they will return all at once.

#6: The child is to blame.

#7: If the attacker didn't penetrate—i.e., rape—the child, then he or she wasn't *really* hurt.

#8: Once survivors reach the point of controlling their emotions, they are all right; they should then begin to put the past behind them and get on with their lives.

#9: Childhood sexual abuse is no big deal. Survivors should just forget about it and get on with their lives.

#10: Their previous silence proves that both child and adult survivors are lying.

#11: Abuse survivors should keep silent.

#12: If survivors lead fulfilling lives, then everything is okay.

#13: Childhood sexual abuse is about sex.

#14: If it only happened once, what's the problem? Survivors live through it, don't they? Why do they allow it to ruin the rest of their lives?

#15: Confrontations are non-threatening and should be a part of every survivor's healing process.

#16: One day the survivor's journey will be over.

#17: The only harm done during sexual abuse is physical; once the body heals, the child heals.

#18: Childhood sexual abuse only affects the child.

#19: We are spending too much time and energy on this issue when few children are actually sexually abused.

Foreword

Everyone who purchases this book does so for a reason. It may be that you are a survivor of childhood sexual abuse. Or perhaps someone close to you—your mate, father or mother, sister or brother, niece or nephew, coworker or best friend ... or your child—is a survivor. Or it may be that recent publicity about this issue has raised your consciousness to the point where you want to learn more about it. Perhaps you are a mental health professional eager to gain a greater feel for the sufferings of the sexual abuse survivors you counsel. Whatever the reason, after reading this book you will begin to understand what at least one woman has gone through.

I am a survivor of childhood sexual abuse. My memories began returning at the age of 34. Twelve years into recovery, after growing stronger and more confident, I chose to share my healing journey. In deciding to write this book, I set three goals.

First, I wanted to assure survivors that what they feel is real and many of those feelings are experienced by other survivors. Although initially many survivors minimize what happened, partly as a means of accepting their reality, eventually they must face the undiminished facts. They must learn there is nothing to be ashamed of. And if they wish to begin the healing journey, they must find the courage to face the whole truth.

Secondly, I wanted to help others understand. In order for anyone (including survivors) to attempt to comprehend the effect of childhood sexual abuse he must understand that this act permeates survivors' lives from the moment of abuse on. It is a part of them, even if they are repressing memories of the abuse. It impacts on every major decision they make, whether or not they remember what happened. It beats through them just as blood beats through every part of their body. There is no escaping it! Realizing that childhood sexual abuse is all-encompassing is fundamental to understanding.

Lastly, I wanted to help educate those who were not abused. The actions and expectations of men and women who have not been sexually violated play a major role in the survivor's ability to accept and heal, especially in the beginning stages when he or she is traumatized and weak. I feel it is important for everyone to appreciate what survivors experience and feel.

This book addresses childhood sexual abuse mainly from a woman's perspective because I draw upon my experiences. However, boys also fall victim to this crime. It is currently estimated that of all children who are sexually abused in childhood, between 30 and 37.5 percent are boys. Generally I refer to my male attacker although I realize women also abuse children. It is currently estimated that of all adults who sexually abuse children, one in ten is a woman. It is my hope that male survivors and their families and friends, and those survivors who were sexually abused by women, will apply what I have written to their own unique situations and use the information as a tool in their healing journey.

Three common themes thread their way through the book. A few words about each of these elements seems in order.

Misconceptions

There are many misconceptions that cloud the issue of childhood sexual abuse. These misconceptions prevent others—even family members and close friends—from understanding the depth and tragedy of this crime. Survivors also buy into these misconceptions, thus preventing themselves from healing. At least one misconception is presented in each chapter; it is then discounted through the material contained therein.

Suggestions for Survivors

The suggestions for survivors presented near the end of each chapter are intended to serve as guidelines, not rules, on goals survivors can work toward as they accept what happened and journey toward recovery. Although survivors must map out their own recovery routes, the paths they follow are similar.

Survivors won't instantly succeed at incorporating these suggestions into their life patterns, but they should measure their success with each small victory. It might help to write the suggestions on 3"x5" cards and read them during the day, or to focus on one suggestion at a time, repeating the chosen goal over and over until it is mastered. The important thing is to recognize the value of setting goals and to work slowly toward achieving them.

Suggestions for Friends and Family of Survivors

These suggestions, presented near the end of each chapter, discuss how family and friends can deal with the knowledge that someone they care about is a survivor and how they can support the survivor.

It is my belief that any form of childhood sexual abuse is harmful, and all survivors must go through similar recovery processes—no matter how long they were abused or what physical form the abuse took. Whether or not a survivor can undertake recovery, and the length of time the healing process will take, is based not only upon the type of sexual abuse suffered but is also influenced by the survivor's own internal resources. A number of dynamics are involved in recovery, including the general functionality of the family in other areas, the length of the molestation, the number of molesters, the support of family if the molestation occurred apart from the family situation, and the severity of the molestation.

It helps to think of molestation as occurring along a very long continuum. A single incident of having a breast grabbed by a stranger in the subway would represent one end of the continuum while 20 years of oral, anal, and vaginal rape by a father would represent the other end of the continuum. The experiences of every survivor fall somewhere along this continuum, but all occurrences are destructive!

Understanding that last sentence—and believing it—is very important, particularly in today's climate where those who would negate survivors' experiences are given press space and air time on talk shows. There is now talk of derailing "the incest-survivor machine" composed of survivors who are trying to convince adults that they were molested as children.

While it is generally agreed that behaviors that include incest and/or rape or other penetration of a child's body are classified as sexual abuse, in fact a far wider range of activities falls into this category. The short definition of *childhood sexual abuse* is "any physical, verbal, visual, or psychological activity of a sexual nature that happens to a child under the age of 18 and makes him or her feel uncomfortable."

The long definition of childhood sexual abuse encompasses (but is not restricted to) the following types of behavior:

- Incest and/or rape or other penetration of a child's body.
- Encouraging or intimidating a child into participating in sex when the child doesn't want to.
- Any type of touching of a child in sexual areas of the body.
- Any sexual activity requested of a child, such as touching an adult in a sexual manner.
- Involving a child in sexual movies or photographs, whether they are required to watch or pose.
- Forcing a child to subject him/herself to prostitution.
- Requiring a child to participate in ritual abuse of a sexual nature.
- Forcing a child to watch others perform sexual acts or to focus on sexual body parts.
- Fondling, kissing, or holding a child in a manner which makes him or her uncomfortable.
- Bathing a child in a manner that is physically or psychologically intrusive.
- Intruding on a child who is bathing.
- Verbal communications that violate a child, such as talking about sex or body parts; ridiculing a child about his or her body. Calling a child a "whore" or "bitch."
- Visual communications that violate a child, such as staring at a child's body or leering in a sexually suggestive manner.

When these behaviors are perpetrated by older children on younger ones—including siblings—it is *still* sexual abuse.

Part of the confusion surrounding behaviors not widely accepted as childhood sexual abuse stems, in part, from misunderstanding a child's behavior when such abuse occurs. Sometimes children will respond positively to being touched. They might be sexually aroused, which feels good to them, or they might be feeling lonely and neglected—and any type of attention relieves this ache. This reaction leads others (particularly abusers) to believe the child liked or even *wanted* to be touched. In fact, children—especially pre-pubescent children—don't understand what is happening to them when they are touched in sexual ways. Often they do not have words to describe their feelings, and they don't understand that they are being abused. Children want and need affection; they don't *ever* want to be abused.

There are control issues involved when children are sexually abused. The abuser is older, bigger, and more knowledgeable. The abuser wields both physical *and* psychological advantages over the child. Often the abuser is someone the child admires. There is no balance between the abuser and the abused ... no even playing field, no chance for the experience to be positive for the child.

* * * * *

One of the first lessons survivors must learn is that their reality doesn't depend on the acceptance of others. Nor does their reality depend on converting disbelievers. The truth just is. My strength has come from recognizing the truth, learning to live with it, and controlling its effect on me instead of allowing it to continue to control me.

In writing about my experiences, I have cloaked myself in one protective device—I use a pen name. But it is a name that is a part of me. Elizabeth is my middle name and Adams is the maiden name of my beloved paternal grandmother. In some ways my pen name is more a part of me than my legal name because it symbolizes my progress. I have come to think of myself as Elizabeth Adams. All other information contained in this book is the truth. Although much of it is based on memories of events that happened over 30 years ago, these returning memories are as clear to me as if they took place moments ago.

Through publishing this book, I want to reach out to other survivors, helping them to accept themselves and begin the journey toward healing. For all those whose lives have been changed by childhood sexual abuse—survivors as well as their friends and family—I strive to offer understanding, encouragement, and hope. By working toward removing the stigma of childhood sexual abuse, I want to help break the cycle so future generations of children will not be plagued by these heinous crimes.

If you are a survivor who has begun to come to terms with your reality, you will recognize yourself time and again as you read this book. Hopefully, my words will give you strength.

If you were not sexually abused as a child, but you accept things can happen that you don't understand, then you will benefit from reading this book. If you approach this task with an open mind, you will, at least momentarily, glimpse the world of survivors.

Two left-handed drawings by Beverley's inner child, done about one month apart. At first, she feels desperately lonely; later, after Beverley has listened to her and comforted her, she feels loved and depicts herself snuggled in Beverley's arms.
Reprinted by permission of the artist, Beverley Spencer, a survivor.

1

In the Beginning

*I am in awe of the little girl I was. I have learned from her
through understanding what she experienced
and what she had to do to survive.*

My early childhood years were darkened by events that taught me
a fear that haunted my days and plagued my nights. Fear that centered
around dark deeds that were so horrible I repressed the memories until
long after I reached adulthood.

When I started working on this book, I couldn't name the exact
time the torment started. It happened after I began to physically
develop (around age 10) and before my sophomore year in high school
(age 14). I chose to conclude the first incident took place when I was
13, probably because I like to think of myself as *not so young* when
it happened. I do not usually think of myself as having participated in
a childhood because I assumed so much responsibility at a young age.
And I gained a degree of comfort from believing the torment began at
the later age because it allowed me to salvage the earliest years in my
memory.

He and his wife lived in our neighborhood and became my
parents' friends. He wasn't tall, but he was strong as an ox. He was
built like a cement truck, with a huge barrel stomach, and his booming
laugh seemed to echo endlessly. His outgoing nature and willingness
to help others drew people to him, and he loved children. Even now
it seems almost inconceivable that this kind, caring man could have
been the inflictor of torment.

One night when he and his wife were visiting, he followed me into the family room. Suddenly, he was upon me and had backed or pushed me against the wall. As one of his hands covered my mouth to prevent me from calling for help, his large body rubbed against mine. His other hand groped at my breasts and then at my crotch as he whispered horrible, suggestive things. I struggled to free myself, but my efforts were useless when pitted against his massive strength.

He warned me not to call out, and then he removed his hand from my mouth and began kissing me. I struggled and turned my head away, but he grabbed my face and forced me to look at him. When his attempts to part my lips failed, he covered my nose. Then he thrust his tongue into my mouth as his penis pounded against my body. With his free hand, he continued to squeeze and claw at my breasts. I wanted to cry out, but I couldn't. As his tongue surged deeper into my mouth, I gagged as I feared he would push it down my throat. It took all my effort just to breathe.

Time seemed to stand still, and I thought the attack would never end. My senses were heightened as everything he did to me, as well as what I felt, was burned into my brain. And then I became removed from the attack as I wondered what was happening in the living room, where my parents, his wife, my two brothers and sister were gathered. I wondered how they could continue their conversation when such awful things were happening to me. Why couldn't they hear his deep breathing or his gruff whispers? Why couldn't they hear his pounding heartbeat or his body thrusting against mine?

And then a new fear crept through me, freezing my mind, gripping my body, and paralyzing me. What if someone saw us? Surely I would be blamed!

Finally his tongue left my mouth and he stared at me. There was no kindness in his eyes. This horrible man was a stranger. He began whispering something about it being my fault, but I just wanted to get away. He restrained me by pushing his body hard against mine, still pinning me to the wall. He put one hand over my mouth and nose, while the fingers of his other hand encircled my throat. As he applied pressure with both hands, inflicting pain and preventing me from breathing, he threatened to kill me if I ever told anyone what had passed between us. And then he threatened to kill my mother.

As I looked into the eyes of the man I had always thought of as the gentle giant, I was consumed with fear. There was no doubt in my mind that he could easily carry out his threats. And as he grinned wickedly and laughed softly, I knew he would enjoy it!

He returned to the living room and again became a part of the happy group. I went to my bedroom and was consumed with such shame, fear, revulsion, and self-loathing as I had never known. I felt I had done something to bring on the attack, that I was to blame. As the hours slowly passed, I feared discovery would destroy my family. I worried about what everyone would think of me if they shared my awful secret. It never entered my mind that he was at fault. Since none of it made sense, how would anyone place the blame on him? I felt dirty and ugly, and I hated myself for allowing it to happen.

I became convinced that he had marked me in such a way that everyone would know what happened. I felt I was branded for life and there was no way the deed could escape detection. Yet, after he and his wife left and I finally, cautiously ventured out of the bedroom, no one treated me differently. I thought they were humiliated by my behavior, that they preferred to pretend nothing had happened for the sake of the family. I wanted to confess, to seek my parents' help. But I couldn't. His threats ensured my silence.

Since I didn't have the strength or resources to cope with the dreadful secret alone, I pushed it deep into my subconscious mind. I never remembered until he and his wife visited our house, or until my family visited their home. But the moment I saw him, all the terrible memories came rushing back. And then I was certain the horrible deed would be detected. How could my parents not see my flushed face, or hear my heart pounding in panic, or tell that I had broken out in a cold sweat? How could they not see my nervousness—and my fear?

But they didn't notice because my behavior was calculated to protect the secret. I feared their detection would destroy my family.

One of the effects of childhood sexual abuse is that the victim loses track of time. Because the child's world becomes fractured and fragmented, events run together. It is impossible for me to determine how many times my abuser touched or taunted me. What I do remember is numerous separate occasions when I encountered his unwanted advances. It may have happened two or three times a year, or six times a year. But it happened whenever I saw him.

Initially I sought to avoid him, thinking he wouldn't dare attack again for fear of being discovered. But I was wrong. He became bolder, announcing his exit instead of silently following me. When I went to the kitchen to pour coffee for the adults, he offered to help. My protests that it wasn't necessary fell on deaf ears. I hurried the task, slapping his hands away and insisting if I didn't return quickly someone would come looking for me. But he backed me into a corner or against a wall. He touched my face and breasts, kissed me, and rubbed his body against mine. And he leered at me as he whispered dirty things to me about what he wanted to do to my body.

I quickly learned safety was gained by surrounding myself with others. I asked one of my brothers or my sister to stay near me during his visits. As we grew older, eventually the boys became unwilling to grant my requests. Luckily my sister, who is considerably younger than I, was more willing to please. Without knowing it, she became my ally and protector.

But there were times when I couldn't cloak myself in that protection. Whenever he caught me alone, he touched and taunted me. He loved the power he exerted over me, and the fear he induced in me. He gained in stature as his physical and verbal abuse continued to strip me of my sense of self.

Once, they visited right after we finished eating dinner and it was my turn to do the dishes. At my parents' instruction, I commenced with the chore. As I went into the kitchen, I closed the sliding door hoping to seal myself away from him. But he boldly followed a few minutes later, saying he would help. He pawed and clawed at me as I tried to shove dishes into his hands. I kept moving evasively in an attempt to prevent my being forced into the family room and backed against the wall.

But he always succeeded because he was bigger, stronger, more powerful than I was. And he always reminded me that I wanted him, that I was to blame for his attraction to me, that I *caused* him to want me. I felt horrible about myself and I was terrified.

As I grew older, his intrusions took on an added dimension. During one of their visits, I received a telephone call from a close male friend. My attacker listened to my end of the phone conversation as he touched me. After I hung up, he physically restrained me from joining my family until I recounted what my friend said. He then asked sexually-oriented questions about the relationship, which I negated. When it became clear that the young man was *not* my boyfriend, he dropped the matter and eventually I escaped. But it was very apparent that he had considered my friend as a rival and he was jealous.

Shortly after I graduated from high school, they visited when I was talking on the telephone with my boyfriend. My attacker stood beside me, touching me, trying to get me to end the conversation. Realizing it was useless to try to gain any privacy, and frustrated in my attempts to evade his wandering hands, I ended the conversation.

I could tell my attacker was angry by the way he looked at me. He then asked all kinds of personal questions about my relationship with my boyfriend as I tried to evade him. How long had we been dating?

What did we do on dates? Did he kiss me? Did he hold me? Did he like my body? Did he feel me up? Did he like to touch my breasts? Did I allow my boyfriend to take liberties with my body that I denied him? Did we have sex? It was an invasive, humiliating encounter.

The last time I saw him, I was 22 years old. He and his wife came to visit one evening when I was in my bedroom studying for a midterm exam. Soon after they arrived, he climbed the stairs and opened my door. I got up from my desk and told him to leave me alone. He laughed as he closed the door behind him. There was something different about him, and I knew this time he would not be content to just touch and verbally torment me.

I felt panic building up inside me. But suddenly I seemed to enter a different dimension as my senses were heightened, and I saw things as if they were happening in slow motion.

He moved forward, grinning, sure of himself, as I backed away. I moved into an area between my bed and the closet, but he still advanced. As he reached out to grab my arm, I jumped up on the bed. My adrenaline was pumping as everything speeded up. I wrenched my arm away before his fingers clamped down, and I ran across the bed. I opened the door and dashed out of the room while he still tried to maneuver his large frame out of the narrow space behind the bed.

Terrified, I realized it had been a close call. If his grasp on my arm had held, I would not have escaped. In the sanctity of my bedroom, there would have been no interruption. I would not have cried out for help because I feared he would eventually retaliate and kill me. If I hadn't escaped, there is no doubt in my mind that he would have raped me. In my hurry to gain safety, I tripped at one of the top steps and slid down the stairs. As I reached the floor, I looked over and saw my parents staring at me. Their expression showed surprise and curiosity, and I feared they had at last discovered my secret.

After their guests left, I expected my parents to question me about what had happened. But they didn't. I was relieved I would be allowed to keep the little that remained of my dignity—I had averted the rape attempt! Again I pushed the memories into my subconscious, where they would remain buried for another 12 years.

Without understanding why, I knew my parents' home was no longer a place where I could be safe. I moved into an apartment, feeling I had to take control of my life and protect myself from some unknown danger. I never thought about the man who had inflicted such harm because I no longer remembered the abuse. But his deeds continued to haunt me as they influenced the direction my life would take.

Twelve years ago, at age 34, my memories began returning. Horrified by what had happened in my youth, I tried to deny, then further suppress them. But it didn't work. Then I tried to minimize and discount what happened to me rather than accepting the resulting devastation. One of the most difficult things for anyone (including survivors) to accept is how sexual molestation can be so destructive to a child. Some people who know about my past have asked how it could have had such a devastating impact on my whole life. Throughout many of the years of my recovery, I could not have answered their questions, but now I understand.

It wasn't just one incident that caused damage, it was the years of continuing terrorization that followed. It wasn't just the attacks against my body that inflicted harm, it was the destruction of my safe world. His actions didn't just inflict physical pain; they robbed me of my psychological, emotional, and spiritual well-being.

Basically, children need to feel safe and secure in their environment, and they need to trust the people who surround them. These elements form the very cornerstone of personality development. When their secure world is shattered by sexual abuse, these children lose all trust—in others and in themselves. They lose all sense of security, comfort, calm. They lose all sense of balance. They feel trapped in a world that is out of control.

Because the attacks occurred in my home, the very base of my secure world, there was no place where I could feel safe. And just as my safe world was shattered, so too was I. I felt like Humpty Dumpty, only I was pushed off the wall. I felt like a glass doll that had been stepped on and crushed; but because I repressed the memories, I didn't know the reason for my feelings.

I turned against myself, hating myself and my body. I felt that I was branded by some evil that dwelled within me. I believed everyone else saw and understood what was wrong with me, yet I didn't know the truth behind my shame. I felt like an "untouchable," undeserving of acceptance and love.

Child survivors feel numb and lost. Cast adrift in a horrifying world, they sense that a part of them has died. They wander through each day feeling as if they exist in a hollow shell. And then the terror returns and the pain is so great that they are plunged into what can only be described as a living hell. All these feelings persist, even if they are repressing the memories of abuse. Is it any wonder that abused children feel like they are dead? Or wish they had died? And yet these children live. They cling to life as if that action alone can defeat their attackers.

Because of the unexplained horror that lived within me, I felt frozen, incapable of feeling, incapable of understanding or escaping my fractured reality. Because my parents were home at the time of the attacks, I felt there was no one who could protect me. Because the attacks were launched by a family friend, I believed there was no one whom I could trust—not even myself because I hadn't prevented the attacks. I lived in fear that the world I knew would be destroyed. Yet I didn't understand the source of my fear.

My personality was crushed during the attacks, and the one I tried so hard to build afterward was formed on a fractured base. I had lost all sense of safety and personal value. Although outwardly I appeared normal, the inner me was hollow, frightened, alone. I was incapable of trusting or of forming solid relationships with others.

The tasks required of sexually abused children are almost impossible to comprehend. They must learn to trust when doing so puts them at risk; they must try to find safety in a world that is *not* safe; they must maintain the appearance of order in a world that is in disarray; they must display control in a situation of helplessness. Such contradictions leave them feeling fragmented.

Because their sense of self is destroyed, they must develop new identities. Upon this crumbling base, child survivors must also form new personalities. The repeated trauma inflicted upon them by their continuing abuse contributes substantially to the development of their personalities— both forming it and *de*forming it.

Hampered by their deformed personalities, abused children must grow into adolescence and adulthood. As the years pass, these children develop the techniques that ensure their survival and protect their horrible secrets, but the fracture in their self-identities intensifies. As the history of abuse becomes deeply integrated into their personalities, as well as embedded into their physical makeup, extensive damage is inflicted on these children.

My initial trauma experience happened near the beginning of my adolescent years, at a time when I should have been expanding my horizons; instead it stunted my ability to grow in appropriate ways. Rather than feeling confident about my abilities, I was tortured; rather than wishing to expand my world, I was terrified of both the familiar and the unfamiliar.

As I entered young adulthood, it seemed I would never be able to establish independence and intimacy because my attempts to grow were *still* colored by the abuse experiences. Even without my conscious knowledge, the events of my childhood abuse influenced the decisions I made and how I felt about other people and about myself.

In order to cope with my reality, I put constraints on myself and the relationships I entered into, limiting how much of the world I was willing to venture into. This action led to a sheltered and restricted life. The tremendous toll extracted by abuse experiences is compounded by the fact that survivors don't understand themselves and they aren't understood by others. This leads to further withdrawal and isolation. And that is exactly what the perpetrator intended!

* * * * *

Misconception #1: Perpetrators can be easily spotted.

It would be comforting if all perpetrators were easily recognized—if they came with a mark on their forehead, or two fingers of their right hand fused together, or wearing a common emblem on their clothes—anything to identify them as the malevolent people they are. Reading the newspaper or watching the news on television confirms that they come in all shapes, sizes, ages, colors; they come from various religious, social, and economic backgrounds; they pursue all sorts of careers.

They even come in both sexes. It is estimated that men are responsible for 80 percent of the incidences of sexual abuse involving boys, while 95 percent of all female victims are abused by men. Which means 20 percent of sexually abused boys and 5 percent of sexually abused girls suffered at the hands of women.

Perpetrators are too sophisticated to be easily spotted through their behavior. Many work hard at becoming pillars of the community, liked and trusted. Others camouflage the truth by appearing ordinary. Perpetrators hope that no one will suspect and, if exposed, no one will believe such a terrible thing about them. Because they are in a position of power—they are older, physically and psychologically stronger, able to inflict terror—they trust their victims will remain silent. And for those same reasons, it is no wonder their victims do remain silent. That silence, coupled with a community predisposed to disbelieve, protects perpetrators from being discovered.

Suggestions for Survivors

- Learn everything you can about childhood sexual abuse.
- Try to understand that your attacker is totally to blame.
- Try to accept that all kinds of people from all walks of life sexually abuse children.
- Try to understand that all abuse experiences are terribly damaging.

Suggestions for Friends and Family of Survivors

- Try to accept that all kinds of people from all walks of life sexually abuse children.
- Try to understand that survivors are never to blame.
- Believe what survivors say about their abuse experiences.
- Learn as much as you can about childhood sexual abuse.
- Try to understand that all forms of sexual abuse are terribly damaging.

Conclusion

For 12 years after my memories began returning, I clung to the belief that the abuse started when I was 13 years old. Recently, additional memories were recovered that allow me to accurately place it at age 10. In a matter of moments, I lost 3 more years of my childhood to a man who was a "family friend."

As my experiences demonstrate, perpetrators cannot be easily spotted. Thus, we must be very careful in making judgments about adults, in order to protect children. And we must take care to understand children, especially considering that abused children almost always disguise the truth to protect themselves and those they care for.

It is my hope that others will benefit from reading about my experiences. There is one message above all that must be heard. Despite the destructive nature of the deeds that were perpetrated against me as a child, I have survived, and I am recovering.

"Like tracking a bear through the snow, you can trace the impact of child sexual abuse across the years of your life. And then you can heal it."
— Margot Silk Forrest, survivor
Editor of *The Healing Woman* newsletter

"I never got to experience the 'maiden' part of my life. That's an incredible loss you can never recapture."
— Leona Tockey, incest survivor and therapist
Interviewed for *The Healing Woman* newsletter

2

The Healing Begins

A light was turned on when the truth was unveiled.
The light became brighter when I embraced the
truth and began to search for myself.

Misconception #2: It is impossible for survivors of childhood
sexual abuse to recover from the trauma of their past.

This misconception is generally held by survivors, especially
during the period of time directly following the retrieval of their initial
memories. The truth is, recovery *is* possible but it takes time and
considerable work on the part of survivors.

Misconception #3: The child could have
prevented the assault.

This is a powerful lie, one that I bought into for years after my
memories returned. I felt old, mature, self-sufficient as I grew into my
teen and early adult years. I stopped viewing myself as a child. And
because I believed I should have prevented the attack, I accepted the
responsibility for it—and the shame.

* * * * *

Being a survivor of childhood sexual abuse is not easy. It entails
being enveloped in fear and surrounded by the unknown, and it
involves feeling rejected and unworthy of love. For those who
repressed memories, recovering the past draws to an end the period of
mystery about themselves, but it ushers in the period of surviving
unimaginable horror and pain.

Before my memories returned, like many survivors, I was haunted by nightmares. Mine contained dark shadows that followed me, reaching out to grab me, making me afraid. For victims of long-term trauma (e.g., survivors of combat, internment in concentration camps, childhood sexual abuse), even when the danger is removed, the threat continues in what, to others, must seem like bizarre and irrational fears. The terrifying emotions experienced by survivors can only be understood if one realizes the horror of these trauma nightmares, which often involve flashbacks. Rather than experiencing dreams that are scary, survivors often relive the horror of their past. It is as if the events are happening again, that their attacker is with them in the present.

When my memories first returned, I was in shock. I wondered how I could wake up each morning, how I would get through each day, how I could continue to perform at my job. I wondered how I would ever survive this horrible knowledge and get on with my life. But as the shock slowly wore off, I was able to assimilate the truth and eventually receive more memories. After I accepted a series of memories and felt I was beginning to successfully deal with the physical elements of the abuse (although I was far from healing), I finally remembered the threats at the end of the attacks.

His brutal death threats ensured that the dark deeds that passed between us would remain our "secret" for over 20 years. They also resulted in psychological damage that, in my opinion, far outweighed the physical harm inflicted. He so successfully instilled terror and helplessness in me that I lost my sense of self. I lost my ability to relate to others when my own safety and peace of mind were concerned. He didn't have to kill me in order to bring about my psychological death. He made me feel my body had died and I existed in an empty shell.

It took me a very long time to deal with the resulting fear I experienced, as an *adult*, even after my attacker was dead. Although it was irrational, I feared he would somehow escape from his grave and make good on his threats because I had finally broken my silence. I was again haunted by nightmares; but this time I was pursued by a man with a face and a name, not a shadow.

Retrieving the memories of childhood sexual abuse is only the first step in a very painful, difficult struggle as survivors walk down the long and lonely path toward recovery. The goal is to move from being victims to becoming survivors to becoming fully functional, multi-dimensional human beings for whom the molestation is only part of their history.

But survivors can't begin working on that goal until they understand nothing they could have done would have prevented the attack. Despite the fact that, as a rational adult, I knew my attacker was responsible, I still blamed myself years after my memories returned. Initially I punished myself unconsciously; then I consciously blamed myself once the memories returned.

Accepting guilt for the attack is practically a universal trait among survivors of childhood sexual abuse, and yet this behavior is hard for those who were not abused to understand. Some professionals in the field of mental health believe survivors may find it easier to blame themselves for not having done enough to prevent the attack(s) than to accept the reality of their utter helplessness at the hands of their attacker.

Often abusers are in positions where they are authority figures (e.g., a teacher, scout leader, priest, coach, or doctor). In cases where the victim admires the abuser, she must also deal with additional conflict. It is very difficult for children to give up their heroes or to admit those they hold in high esteem can do bad things. Often exposure will bring about the additional threat of losing something they desire (e.g., getting a good grade, earning a badge, making the team).

When my nephew visited from out of state when he was 13, I focused on his lack of sophistication, innocence, fragile build, and youth. I knew almost any woman who wanted to sexually abuse him would have succeeded. The element of surprise would have gained the advantage; her superior strength would have carried out the deed. After observing my nephew, I was able to see myself as his counterpart. Once I accepted that I was a *child* when the abuse took place, I understood nothing I could have done would have prevented my abuser from succeeding with the initial attack. Even if I had advance knowledge of what was coming—which I did not—my inferior strength would have prevented me from protecting myself against the assault.

I finally realized my attacker had taken my childhood from me and at last I appropriately placed the blame on *him*. Only then did I begin to heal.

It is important to note that, although a child cannot prevent an unexpected assault, speaking up *after* an attack is another matter entirely. If I had summoned the courage to tell my parents what happened, the following 12 years of terrorization might have been prevented.

Survivors go through similar stages as they strive for healing. Some of the stages they must go through are: the search for understanding; mourning over what was taken; grief for a childhood lost; proper placement of blame and rage; and finally, acceptance of what is. It is a frightening process, especially the reclaiming of emotions. Often I felt out of control, and I hated the feelings that welled up within me. But I had to give in to them in order to heal.

As I consciously made the decision to recover, I drew comfort from the fact that I was not alone. I drew courage from reading about other women who share my experiences. And I drew strength from finding the label that describes me—*survivor*. As I have moved toward healing, I have learned the recovery process can take years— or a lifetime. At the end of the journey, survivors know they are not like those who were not molested; but if they are lucky, through their search they have also learned they are not alone.

This partially describes what I have experienced as I waged a mostly private battle, coming to terms with my past and accepting the truth of how, on an unconscious level, the abuse has constantly affected my life. At the time it happened, there were no support groups or television shows that warned children about the threat of being sexually abused by a family friend. It occurred during an age of silence, yet such abuse was always around ... always happening. I dealt with it in silence at the time of the abuse and during my initial adult attempts to heal—in silence and with deep fear.

But at last I understood the nightmares that had plagued me at various stages of my life, nightmares that became my constant late-hour companions. And slowly I became acquainted with the stranger whom I had often felt shared my body—the stranger who had made decisions for me, guided me, and somehow protected me by placing me in safe situations. I had never feared the stranger. Now that I understood why, it was time to come to terms with my past, integrate all the pieces of the puzzle that was my life, and understand all the inconsistencies and conflicts that were a part of me.

After the shock of the returning memories began to wear off, all these inconsistencies made sense. And as more memories returned, I began to realize how fragile my existence was. Before I knew the truth, I had felt fragmented, incomplete, hollow, drained, unable to feel; much of the time I was a stranger even to myself. Now I felt like my life was a kaleidoscope worked by unseen hands. All I had to do was free my brain, enabling it to be receptive to information about the past, and then this horrible knowledge came to me—too bright, confused, swirling out of my control.

In the fragmented stage, there had been a lot of blanks and a certain amount of mystery; there was loneliness, but no acute pain. In this new puzzle stage, there was more intense pain than I had ever imagined. Initially, with the unveiling of new memories, I felt as if my heart had been pierced by the jagged glass edges of the pieces of the puzzle as they fit into place, and blood gushed out of my body. I wondered how anyone could survive under such conditions. Why didn't I just die? I felt so fragile that at times I feared I would shatter into a thousand tiny pieces, never to be put back together again.

Later, as the puzzle pieces began to rapidly slip into place, I felt as if my heart had been pricked by several sharp edges and my life force was slowly oozing out of the tiny holes. At times I believed I would have done anything to return the memories, to regain the comfort of being encased in the fog that had shrouded my past instead of having to face the horror of the reality that was my life. But that wasn't an option. Once consciousness had been raised, I couldn't go back to the state of ignorance. When I was a child and young adult, repression of the memories was a key to my survival. Now I had to learn that facing the memories was the key to recovery and healing. And as I faced the truth, I began to understand my life and my self.

I could sometimes control the flow of memories by keeping my mind constantly occupied; then, suddenly, something would trigger them and I would fall into the dark hole of my past. But at last I reached the point where I needed to make myself whole, and I chose to face the shadows that haunted my nightmares. I used writing as a tool in my recovery process. Ironically, it was also the instrument through which I had enhanced my self-esteem, and it was the instrument that set the stage for triggering the return of the initial memories.

During the early years of recovery, writing provided a medium where I felt safe, where I could explore my feelings and thoughts. It also became the means through which, at times, I escaped my reality. Initially I wrote non-fiction, through which I explored the non-sexual issues that were a part of me. Then I wrote fiction as a means of dealing with my torment and exploring all the thoughts and feelings that had been buried deep inside me. I also explored sexual issues in the safe context of the actions of my characters—first dealing with adolescents and then adults. Through my characters, I was able to explore in a safe way. I was able to pretend it wasn't really me I was dealing with, but *them.*

I became practically possessed. Every free second of time was spent writing. Sometimes I wrote for over 40 hours each weekend, and I wrote from 6:00 p.m. until midnight every night after coming home from work. Over a period of 5 years, I completed rough drafts of fifteen novels and four volumes of short stories totalling over 12,000 pages. It wasn't necessary to perfect any of them; I just had to get the ideas down, to complete the plots, to draw the characters. Finishing those manuscripts would come later, when I was more at peace with myself. It was a painful process, especially when I was unable to manipulate the characters and when I had to confront their emotions. And I could not avoid using the words *breast, her center*, and *his throbbing member*, all of which called up what had happened to me so long ago.

After years of writing fiction, at last I wrote a short story titled "Buried Too Deep." Although the heroine is named Christina, the setting is fictional, and the story contains many scenes that never occurred in my life, it is really about what happened to me.

Now I know the same was true of all my writing. No matter who the characters were or what happened to them, my writing had one purpose. It helped me grow to the point where I was able to deal with my past, accept the truth, come out of the darkness of fear and repression, and bathe myself in the light of truth and understanding.

This process allowed me to mourn for what was taken from me— my childhood, innocence, joy, trust, security, pride, self-esteem, pleasure in myself and my body. It allowed me to go through the agony of blaming myself until I was able to accept that I had done nothing to bring on the assault. It allowed me to feel anguish until finally I knew I couldn't have prevented the attack. And at last it allowed me to reach the point of rage as I finally placed full responsibility where it belonged—*on him.*

During this process, I learned recovery and healing cannot be rushed by the survivor or caring others. Survivors must set a slow pace, choosing to move cautiously when it's warranted. This isn't easy, especially at the beginning, but it is worth the effort expended in asserting the necessary control. Once the memories return, survivors often expect their adult persona to dictate instant healing. When that fails, they feel defeated. They blame themselves, often minimizing and discounting the seriousness of what happened to them.

Survivors also expect to move quickly and constantly toward recovery. They don't realize that recovery is a slow process, with stops and starts. There will be times when survivors are not ready to address their recovery, when they bury themselves in work, when they keep occupied every waking moment. There will be periods of physical and mental exhaustion, when continuation of recovery is simply not possible.

These interludes are a necessary part of healing. They provide time for survivors to look back on what they have accomplished, to assess the current situation, and to gather strength for the next step. During this period of time, survivors will feel a wide range of emotions ranging from relief and satisfaction for the progress they have made to rage and devastation over the harm inflicted on them by their abuser. I have experienced all these things during my journey toward healing.

In the 12 years since my memories began returning, I have had many positive and negative experiences involving disclosure and my recovery. It's easy to incorporate the positive feedback and move ahead. But with each negative experience, I suffered a degree of setback. However, I have always been able to learn from those negative experiences and to use them in eventually moving forward with my recovery.

In recent years, when television shows and newspaper articles have explored the issue of childhood sexual abuse, I have seen that what I went through is standard procedure for survivors. Through reading about other survivors, I received confirmation that, given the parameters of my life, I am normal.

When I began my healing journey, it was widely believed that one in seven women of my generation were victims of childhood sexual abuse. Today that figure is conservatively placed at one in three, while it is estimated that one in five to seven men were sexually abused in childhood. As in my case, many survivors lead outwardly normal lives, the horror of their past masked by their tremendous drive to succeed and prove themselves. As in my case, many survivors never report the crime perpetrated against them, nor do they seek professional help in healing.

Each survivor must come to terms with the issue of counseling on his own. Seeking professional help puts survivors in contact with therapists who are trained to deal with the aftermath of sexual abuse. Further, through participating in group therapy, survivors meet other men and/or women who share their experiences.

My decision not to seek counseling was based on the strong sense that I was moving in the right direction, possibly because of my training in psychology. Also, I have utilized informal counseling opportunities through developing personal relationships with two therapists who talk with me about my past, and I lead staff self-help groups at work that allow me to focus on my healing. Despite the progress I have made, I am becoming more aware that recovery would have been easier, quicker, and less lonely if I had sought professional help at the beginning of the journey. I haven't ruled out this possibility for the future.

Survivors should select a tool for dealing with their healing. They might keep a journal, write letters to their abuser that they never mail (or that they do mail), or compose poetry to express their feelings. Some survivors choose to paint or draw, or to sew a quilt. Whatever tool they select, they should make sure it focuses on their feelings and allows them to look back and chart their progress.

When survivors are ready to share their recovery with others, they should try to build a strong network of empathetic people who will support and assist during recovery. This isn't easy to do. It takes careful thought, time, and the willingness of others to give of themselves in a very difficult situation. It also takes a lot of luck. In attempting to build a network, survivors risk exposure and rejection. However, succeeding in constructing such a network provides a safety net for survivors.

This network can be built near the beginning of recovery or farther along in the healing process. I chose the latter. After spending years dealing with my torment in secluded silence, at last I wanted to know that I was no longer alone and I needed an outlet for expressing my pain. I found what I required in a group of carefully selected, caring female colleagues. (Not family members, not my closest personal friends.)

In the safety of my trusted circle, I was able to experience my worth as a human being. I was also able to measure my progress through listening to their observations. But most of all, I was uplifted by their understanding, acceptance, and love. As I grew stronger and was again able to focus on other things, this circle of women became far more than my recovery unit. They are now an integral part of my whole life, and I count them among my closest friends.

I finally decided to go public with my story because the tragedy of childhood sexual abuse touches so many men and women—and their families, friends, mates, children, generation after generation. At first, I didn't know what form my public disclosure would take; but I knew the next stage of my recovery would entail reaching out to others, and I sensed it had something to do with my writing.

I felt responsible for sharing my experiences. I couldn't wipe out the memory of a friend's words when I trusted her with my secret and she responded, "It happened to me, too; I am a freak!" I was the only person she had confided in, and I got the distinct impression her disclosure was an accident. Her pain mirrored my own, but I believe her torment was greater because she intended to carry the burden alone. I realized she was still a victim, not a survivor. Through my journey, I have learned that some of the keys to survivors coping with and eventually healing after such trauma are sharing, learning they are not alone, and understanding others have had similar experiences and share many of the same feelings.

In February 1992, I read an announcement introducing a new women's newsletter called *The Healing Woman*. The editor, Margot Silk Forrest, was looking for articles written by women who had personal or professional experience with childhood sexual abuse. I wrote to her, telling some of my personal history, suggesting possible articles I could submit, and enclosing a check for a subscription. Although it had not yet gone to press, I had a strong feeling this publication was something I needed. Her response to my query changed my life.

While writing articles for *The Healing Woman*, I read portions of a few books on childhood sexual abuse. I found a wealth of information that backed up everything I had experienced; they confirmed that I had gone through appropriate stages while traveling along the path to recovery. And I was now in touch, by phone, with two therapists and an editor—three women who understood, cared, were willing to share, and were devoting their professional lives to helping adult survivors. In talking with them, it was as if we had known each other for years, and I felt as if I were being hugged by the person at the other end of the line. At last I truly felt I was not alone.

As I focused on every detail of what happened to me so long ago, I uncovered memories that might have remained buried in my subconscious. One of the most recent memories retrieved concerned an assault by a second man when I was 20 years old. Reclaiming the additional memories wasn't easy, but it was necessary.

In May 1992, the first issue of *The Healing Woman* arrived. Excited, I stopped what I was doing and read it from cover to cover. I laughed, I cried, I felt warm inside. And then I sat very still, in awe, as a deep calm encompassed me. Here, at last, was confirmation of my existence. I was splashed across those pages, and it felt good because it meant everything I had felt and experienced was real. And I am okay. I was so deeply moved by *The Healing Woman* that I sent subscription information to friends who are also survivors.

Since reading and writing for *The Healing Woman*, I have become much more vocal about the issue of childhood sexual abuse, and more willing to discuss my own experiences. I have publicly disclosed at my place of work, knowing the risk I was taking. It had always been a *safe* place for me, where my past was unknown and where I felt no shame. Through talking about my experiences, I have realized that silence is unhealthy for survivors, because it allows the stigmas of guilt and shame to remain attached to those who were the *victims*.

Suggestions for Survivors

- Learn everything you can about childhood sexual abuse.
- Accept the fragmented nature of your returning memories and try not to further suppress them.
- Work on understanding that you could not have prevented what happened.
- Set your own pace, allowing yourself to move cautiously and slowly toward recovery.
- Allow time to go through all the appropriate stages of recovery.
- Try to believe you will somehow find the strength to endure.
- Try to accept that the label *survivor* applies to you.
- Work on trusting your instincts.
- Work on accepting your inconsistencies.
- Allow yourself to feel whatever you feel about the abuse and your abuser(s).
- Find a positive outlet for your recovery (e.g., writing, drawing) that allows you to measure your progress.
- Try to learn from both positive and negative experiences.
- Seek professional help and surround yourself with a support network of caring people.
- Learn to accept that you are not alone.
- Try to release the stigmas of guilt and shame.
- Try to make the decision to recover and heal.

Suggestions for Friends and Family of Survivors

- Learn as much as you can about childhood sexual abuse.
- Try to accept that survivors are not to blame.
- Try to accept that survivors are telling the truth about their abuse experiences.
- Try to accept the survivor's sometimes confusing behavior.

Conclusion

Now, many years into my healing journey, I am convinced the ideas expressed in Misconceptions #2 and #3 are false. It *is* possible to recover from childhood sexual abuse. It isn't easy or painless, and it doesn't happen unless the survivor is willing to spend a great deal of time on recovery. But it *can* be done. Further, after years of struggling with self-blame, even when rationally I knew it was not my fault, I finally learned there is nothing I could have done to prevent the attack. Acceptance of these truths gave me the chance to continue with my recovery.

Those who are just beginning to face the truth of their histories of abuse are luckier than I was because now there is a great deal of information available to help them understand and accept the past. Through reading about childhood sexual abuse, survivors can embrace the knowledge that unlocks the mysteries of their past and incorporate into their lives the power that comes from knowing the truth. In doing so, they embrace themselves.

Through my connection with *The Healing Woman*, my personal journey has taken a new direction—one that is focused. It has allowed me to look back and see the path I've walked along during the last 12 years, to measure my progress, and to see where I'm going. It has given me new strength and energy, which is now poured into editing all those rough drafts of manuscripts written so long ago. But most of all, through sharing experiences with other survivors, I now look ahead to the future with hope. I have redefined myself. I understand that, though my journey is not over, I truly am a healing woman.

> *"The spiritual journey is one of continually falling on your face,*
> *getting up, brushing yourself off, looking sheepishly*
> *at God and taking another step."*
> – Sri Aurobindo
> Indian seer and poet

> *"It seems somewhat a miracle that a few of us are*
> *able to fight and claw our way out of the trenches*
> *to discover a sun that lights our way."*
> – Donna Montegna
> *Prisoner of Innocence*

3

Meeting the Beloved Stranger Within

*When I was a child, I lost the ability to love, to feel,
to feel safe, and to trust. When these sensibilities were
taken away, I felt there was nothing left but an empty shell.
Later, I learned that within that empty shell resided the
child who survived the horror of sexual abuse.
Eventually, I learned to value, honor, and love her.
In doing so, I learned to value, honor, and love myself.*

Misconception #4: Survivors can't really block from their
memory what happened to them in childhood.

Actually the blocking takes place in childhood because they
cannot deal with what happened to them. As a means of self-
preservation, they push the memories into their subconscious until
they are able to cope. Some degree of memory repression is virtually
universal among survivors of childhood sexual abuse. Often the
memories don't return until long after survivors reach adulthood. In
my case, the memories began returning when I was 34 years old. With
women, often the memories return when they bear a child or when
their child reaches the age they were when the abuse occurred.

As the following personal experience demonstrates, blocked
memories can have a far-reaching effect on survivors' lives.

* * * * *

There have been many times in my life when I have made
decisions that puzzled me, some of which even alienated those close
to me and seemed to turn me into a stranger. And yet I felt the decisions
were right—the only ones I could make. I learned not to question, but

to trust the inner power that guided me. It was as if my life were being steered by some kind of automatic pilot, a device that was set to protect me from a deep dark secret that had the ability to destroy.

One such decision made 20 years ago—to have an abortion—was particularly painful. I was 26 years old, and had been happily married for 4 years when birth control failed. Although we were pinched for money and living in an apartment, we would have coped with a baby. Although morning sickness struck any time I smelled food, and I changed from a robust-looking woman to a skeletal shadow of myself, I could have coped with this, too. But there was one thing I couldn't cope with: I was plagued by recurring nightmares of dark shadows that followed me.

I remember two nightmares in particular. In the first, I was enveloped by a fog so dense I couldn't see anything around me. I turned and turned, trying to determine in which direction to move to escape the fog or to find something familiar that would tell me where I was. Suddenly I heard footsteps coming toward me and the deep breathing of someone pursuing me. I took a step away from the sound, and the dark shadow of a man's hand reached out to grab me. I quickly averted the hand and, thinking the fog was somehow playing tricks with sounds, moved in the opposite direction. Again the shadow of the hand tried to grab me.

Throughout the dream, I tried to find a way to escape from the shadow, but I could not. No matter which direction I turned in, the hand was there, reaching out for me. As my panic escalated, a man's ugly, tormenting laughter surrounded me and filled me with terror. When the laughter finally subsided, the fog slowly disappeared. No one was there.

The second nightmare was even worse. I wandered through a long, dark tunnel—one so long I couldn't see any light at the end. As I slowly tried to find the end of the tunnel, I felt the wall with my hands as my feet followed the path of train tracks. Suddenly I felt the tracks jiggling under me, and then I heard the rumbling sound of an approaching train. I panicked because the sound echoed in the tunnel, and I couldn't tell which direction the train was coming from. I didn't know which way to run to save myself. Terrified, I ran to my right, and finally I could see some light. But the exit was blocked by a man's huge shadow.

Consumed with fear of him, I turned and ran in the opposite direction. When I finally saw the light, it was again blocked by the shadow. As he moved toward me, I changed direction; then, I stumbled and fell onto the train tracks. As he approached, his tormenting laughter filled the tunnel. At last I knew there was no train, that this horrible man whom I could not identify presented the only danger. As he reached out to touch me, the dream ended. His identity remained a secret.

As the nightmares ended, I woke up bathed in my own icy sweat, shivering, my heart pounding. Throughout most of my life I had been plagued by these types of bad dreams, but now it was different. For the first time, I experienced flashbacks of these strange nightmares during the day. I didn't know the dreams were trying to unmask the fact that I had been sexually molested during my childhood. All I knew was the nightmares were connected with the pregnancy, and I had to stop them.

Abortion was legal at the time, but emotionally it was a very painful decision: I'd felt a strong bond with the 7-week-old being inside me. And physically it was devastating. There were complications during the operation and my heart stopped beating. I tried to call out, but my lips wouldn't move and I had no voice. I tried to reach out to the doctor and nurse to warn them something was wrong, but I couldn't move my arms. I began to panic because I could do nothing to help myself.

Suddenly I realized I was no longer in my body; instead, I was hovering above it. I was able to watch myself and the others, and I knew my life was slipping away.

The nurse turned and looked at my body and motioned to the doctor. Without exchanging a word, they jumped into action. Fortunately, the procedure was being performed in a hospital and everything needed was at hand. That team of health care professionals worked desperately to revive me. Their skill literally saved my life.

Years later, during a period of intense self-examination connected with writing a diet book that was partly based on personal experiences, the dark shadows parted and the terror of my past was revealed. Over the next months, as I remembered the specific details of the horror that had been a part of my childhood, I began to understand all the things that had puzzled me about my behavior: the decisions I had made, the path my life had taken. And suddenly, with clarity, I understood the reason why I had to have that abortion. If I had carried the baby to full term, the physical and emotional changes experienced during pregnancy and birth would have triggered the memories of the past at a time when I was unable to cope with them. The repressed memories of the sexual abuse were represented by the dark shadows that had followed me in my nightmares all those years.

Since many women begin retrieving memories of childhood sexual abuse during pregnancy or when they are considering having an abortion, there appears to be a link between these women's issues. I suspect these women retrieve their childhood abuse memories too soon—before they are psychologically strong enough to deal with them.

Making the decision to have an abortion was difficult, but it was something I believe I had to do. I don't think many women reach this decision easily. It's also not something women simply dismiss once the operation is over. I think about how different my life would be if I'd had that baby. I wonder what my child would have been like and what he or she would want to grow up to be. I think about it when I see children who are the age my child would now be.

In thinking back on that difficult time when I chose to have an abortion, I am painfully aware of how hard it was to make such a serious decision—particularly because, once completed, the deed could not be reversed. Making that decision marks just one of the many times I chose without understanding why and yet knowing it was the right thing for me to do. Although trusting—in others as well as in myself—is very difficult for me, one of my survival techniques was to learn to trust something inside me that I didn't understand. Ultimately, unconsciously I trusted in something I could not consciously define.

That was an important step because trust is a key issue for survivors. Because of the events that took place when they were children, survivors no longer understand what trust is; therefore, they are unable to build trust. Because of their fears, and the feeling they were to blame for what happened, survivors don't trust themselves. Yet during childhood they took the necessary steps to survive the ordeal and to continue living. As adults, they must learn self-trust if they are going to heal.

Throughout all the years when I felt that a stranger occupied my body and made decisions for me, I survived. And I learned to trust that stranger. In recent months, as I read books written by experts in the field of childhood sexual abuse, I was amazed at how often what I read paralleled what I felt or experienced—not just on major issues, but even concerning the minutest details. Over time, I learned to always follow the inner voice of the stranger. Now I know that voice belongs to my subconscious self. It spoke with full knowledge of my past, offering guidance and protecting me.

Suggestions for Survivors

- Try to accept the puzzling parts of your life.
- Try to accept that your fears are real and there are reasons for your nightmares and insecurities.
- Try to accept that childhood sexual abuse impacts on many aspects of your life.
- Work on learning to trust your instincts.
- Try to understand that your primary function (both consciously and unconsciously) was to survive.
- Try not to discount the influence your subconscious had on the decisions you made before your memories returned.
- Try to remember you are not alone.

Suggestions for Friends and Family of Survivors

- Recognize the courage it takes for victims of childhood sexual abuse to survive.
- Try not to condemn survivors for the decisions they make; instead, support them.
- Try to accept that survivors' seemingly irrational fears are very real to them.
- Learn as much as you can about childhood sexual abuse.
- Try to earn the trust of survivors through your supportive behavior.

Conclusion

After spending the last 12 years struggling with and learning to accept the truth of my history of childhood sexual abuse, I know (contrary to the idea expressed in Misconception #4) the memories were repressed without my knowledge in order to protect me. I also know that recovering the memories before I was ready to deal with them would have resulted in physical and/or emotional breakdown, and it probably would have cost me my life. I bless the inner power that guided and protected me from the things I couldn't afford to remember. And I now understand I could not proceed with bringing a new life into the world until I had mothered and learned to love my inner child, for that beloved stranger within was myself.

*"What lies behind us and what lies before us are tiny matters
compared to what lies within us."*
— Ralph Waldo Emerson

*"As soon as you trust yourself,
you will know how to live."*
— Johann Wolfgang von Goethe

4

Returning Memories:
Real or Imagined?

*Out of the deepest, darkest hours of the night comes the
dawn. Out of the deepest, darkest hours of my night
came the dawning of truth.*

Misconception #5: If the returning memories are real,
they will return all at once.

This is simply not true! Actually, memories are usually released
in pieces, giving survivors fragments of the truth of their past. This
chapter, which presents an overview of returning memories and
includes a discussion of the controversy surrounding this issue,
illustrates why Misconception #5 is false.

* * * * *

Survivors of childhood sexual abuse are engulfed by horrible
emotions. They experience feelings of self-hated, rejection, and being
unworthy of love. The lives they lead are fragmented, mysterious, and
hollow. For those who repressed their memories, as I did, recovering
the past draws to an end the period of mystery, but it ushers in the
period of surviving unimaginable horror and pain.

Before my memories returned, like many survivors, I was haunted
by nightmares containing dark shadows. These nightmares hinted at
the dark secrets that were buried in my subconscious. Once my
memories returned, my history of abuse became an almost all-
consuming factor in my life. It seemed to eat me up, to occupy all my

strength, energy, and consciousness. It almost paralyzed me, yet I continued to function.

This element is hard for those who were not abused to understand. It is one reason why those close to survivors become frustrated with the negative changes they see in the behavior of survivors who are beginning to cope with the truth. It also accounts for the perception that survivors who are struggling with their past are not making progress toward recovery. Those who were not abused find it difficult to understand what long, slow processes recovery and healing are.

Initially, I tried to continue to block the memories, then to discount the damage inflicted. But I couldn't stop them from coming. As time passed and the shock slowly wore off, I finally accepted the truth. I reached a stage where I had to try to understand everything about my past in order to understand the ways the abuse had molded the person I became, and to try to reduce the effect the past would have on my future. I believe my recovery and healing began the moment I mounted this conscious effort to deal with my history of abuse.

I opened myself up to receive the memories; I didn't force them, but I no longer blocked them. They came because at that point in time I was strong enough to deal with them. Sometimes I could identify the triggering factor; at other times, I had no idea why they were called forth. Scattered memories about the attack itself returned one piece at a time. But the pieces always fit together until the full picture of that horrible night became known. Then I received memories of the following 12 years of terrorization and attempts to repeat the attack.

At the time, I couldn't talk about what was happening to me. I couldn't put into words what I was "receiving" through the returning memories, or what I was feeling. The emotions—fear, revulsion, self-hated, distrust—were so intense that I felt I would choke if I tried to speak about them. And my thoughts and memories were so fragmented that I suspect anyone who listened to me trying to explain would think I was possessed or crazy.

My memories returned over a period of many years. But each fragment was bright, very distinct and returned with such clarity that I knew it was real. There was no dream-like quality to these returning memories. At no time did I doubt their truth. They filled in the missing pieces of my life, without which I felt puzzled, fractured, lonely, vulnerable. Retrieving the memories allowed me to understand my pain. Being able to make sense of my life eventually allowed me to cope with and finally accept the tragedy of my past.

Drawing upon my experiences, it appears the more damaging memories return at long intervals, after the survivor has dealt with previous memories and is moving toward healing. Each time the most severe memories returned, I experienced a setback; but after accepting the new information, there was continuation of healing.

It is my firm belief that the subconscious does not allow more to surface than the survivor is ready to deal with, although I have often felt I couldn't handle it and frequently reverted to the nightmare stage. In time, I gained the strength to accept the new memories, and I was able to move ahead with my life.

"False" Memories

Before discussing the "false" memory controversy, I want to be very clear about the following point. This book is not based on memories that were retrieved during therapy. It wasn't until after I began writing about my personal experiences with recovery that I spoke to therapists about the issue of childhood sexual abuse. Through those conversations, I received substantiation of everything I had experienced. And I gained comfort from knowing my recovery has progressed in appropriate stages.

Armed with my belief in the truth of my past, I was shocked and troubled when "experts" began appearing on talk shows and writing articles about "false" memories of childhood sexual abuse. Although these charges didn't shake my belief in the truth of my memories, I was outraged that anyone would so openly express disbelief of child victims of such a heinous crime as sexual abuse.

As I investigated the matter through reading numerous newspaper articles, I discovered many of these "experts" are connected either personally or professionally to those who have been accused of committing such crimes. Common sense told me to remain calm. Would my attacker have admitted his guilt if I had confided in my parents and they had confronted him? It's not likely! Would his wife have taken my side against her husband? I doubt it. Using my knowledge of the family circumstances surrounding the man who abused me, it isn't hard for me to imagine that few people who are accused of childhood sexual abuse will, even when confronted with irrefutable evidence, admit their guilt.

The same holds true for the partners of child abusers. In many cases, particularly those involving in-home abuse, the partners know about the abuse and choose to ignore it. Various reasons are offered for such behavior—they didn't want to put the stability of the family at risk, they could not afford to leave the abuser, they overlooked the abusive behavior "for the sake of the children." None of these explanations ever excuses the abuse or the partner's willingness to overlook it.

I learned about a Philadelphia organization called the False Memory Syndrome Foundation. Established in 1992, this organization's purpose is to research and collect information on families who say their adult children have falsely accused them of childhood sexual abuse. The cases targeted by this foundation generally involve memories recovered during therapy, which can include hypnosis, presumably with the implication that the abuse memories were "triggered" by the suggestions of the therapists and are, in fact, false.

Fearing that the flood of recent publicity on "false" memories would endanger the recovery of survivors who are only beginning to come to grips with their past, and shake the confidence of those who had a firm belief in the truth, I was heartened to learn that an appropriate authoritative body had already begun to address this issue. At its Annual Meeting held in San Francisco, California, in May 1993, the American Psychiatric Association began a dialogue on "false" memories.

At a forum titled "Adult Memories of Childhood Trauma: Current Controversies," Judith Herman, M.D. and John Briere, Ph.D. presented position papers addressing the issue of traumatic memories.[1] They spoke of their concern for families and communities when accusations result from the retrieving of "false" memories. They also addressed the dangers to individual child and adult survivors when true memories are ignored. Based on research involving their clients, they presented data that validate survivors' returning memories.

In addressing the issue of why there is such an outcry regarding "false" memories after society initially accepted the concept of repressed memories, Dr. Briere offered, "It is my impression that ... survivors' subsequent involvement in the legal system, both in terms of civil suits and criminal actions against their alleged perpetrators, has lead to a substantial backlash...." *(Briere, page 3)* In fact, the False Memory Syndrome Foundation hires "experts" to testify in court for the defense in cases involving alleged sexual abuse.

Speaking from my own experience, I wouldn't want those who were not sexually abused as children to believe it happened to them. I wouldn't wish such torment on anyone! Further, I believe all professionals who are suspected of abusing their positions of trust by encouraging clients' "false" memories of sexual abuse should be thoroughly investigated by the appropriate licensing body. If the allegations are determined to be true, the authorities should take appropriate action.

However, from what I have been able to ascertain, the number of false accusers is extremely small compared to the number of men and women who were sexually abused in childhood. My fear is that the public exposure given to this small percentage of cases will undermine the good that has been done in the last few years as survivors have begun to publicly break their silence. For those who have never experienced such abuse, make no mistake about it—childhood sexual abuse is damaging on many levels; the returning memories are real; and survivors cannot continue to suppress the truth if they are going to heal.

In the end, I had to allow all the memories to come forth so I could put together the pieces that, up until my recovery period began, represented my fragmented self. Binding those pieces together, coupled with acceptance of the facts, has been part of my healing process. No one—not even the "experts" who are disbelievers—can take that away from me. Not through their ignorance. Not through their charges of lies. Not through their rejection.

* * * * *

Knowing that childhood sexual abuse is a crime that is usually enacted in private, and that perpetrators go to great lengths to protect the awful secret, I was astonished to learn the results of recent research concerning verification of adult survivors' reports of childhood sexual abuse. In her position paper, Dr. Herman wrote, "At a time of their choosing, most of the women in our groups (47/53) actively sought additional information to help them make sense of what they remembered.... When these patients chose to search, most were able to find some independent confirmation of the abuse (83% of those who made the attempt, or 74% of the total)." *(Herman, pages 4-5)*

I was also astounded at the type of confirming evidence Dr. Herman's clients found years after the abuse took place, especially considering that childhood sexual abuse has generally been regarded as a "perfect" crime: "Some [patients] found physical evidence, others obtained an admission from the perpetrator, still others obtained confirmation from another family member or another victim of the same perpetrator." *(Herman, page 5)* In this study, the ability to obtain corroborating evidence was not affected by whether the women had always retained their memories of abuse or had retrieved their memories at a later time.

Although Judith Herman's sample size is small, I believe the percentage of survivors who found proof of the abuse provides convincing evidence of the truth of repressed memories. At the time of the conference, Dr. Herman's findings represented the only systematic study presented in the literature.

Dr. Briere also reported on the research he conducted with Jon Conte involving 450 men and women who were in outpatient treatment for sexual-abuse-related difficulties: "... fifty-nine percent reported having had some period before age 18 when they had had no knowledge of being abused." Further, they found that "... self-reported abuse-related amnesia was associated with more severe and extensive abuse that occurred at a relatively earlier age." *(Briere, page 2)*

Because the issue of childhood sexual abuse is so painful, and the idea of returning memories is so difficult to comprehend, the controversy surrounding abuse memories may continue for some time; meanwhile, people's lives hang in the balance. But at least now survivors can take comfort in knowing there is scientific evidence that backs up their experiences.

Coping with Trauma

Children employ a variety of methods in coping with the trauma of childhood sexual abuse. Often they will employ a series of techniques, depending on the needs of the moment. The following sections touch on a few of these coping mechanisms, all of which I have used (either consciously or unconsciously) to survive.

Dissociation—Dissociative responses are described by Dr. Briere as "... depersonalization and derealization, cognitive disengagement, emotional numbing, or out-of-body experiences, or ... amnesia for painful abuse-related memories." *(Briere, page 1)* Dissociation is a very successful tool for ensuring survival and some children unconsciously become masters at implementing this technique. Studies have proven that there is a correlation between the severity of the trauma and the degree to which children dissociate.

Although the positive side to dissociation is obvious—the child would like to believe the abuse didn't occur—it does not follow that what one doesn't remember can't harm. Survivors often ignore intense pain or symptoms of illness because of their dissociative capabilities.

However, not all children who were sexually abused dissociate; and those who do repress the memories are, at times, incapable of sustaining the blocking. My memories were hidden until my abuser visited. Then the horror of the past rushed through me, creating fear that at times paralyzed me. After he left, I again repressed the memories. They remained buried from age 22 (the last time I saw him) until age 34.

Altering the abuse experience—If the memories of abuse are not repressed, often children employ psychological defenses that alter the abuse experience. This involves either intentionally blocking the memories from conscious awareness, allowing the child to deny the abuse, or negating it by minimizing what happened, allowing the child to accept a piece of the unacceptable.

Self-blame—When children are unable to alter their reality through dissociation or denying the severity of the act that was inflicted upon them, they blame themselves. However, as in my case, even children who are repressing the abuse memories blame themselves—they just don't remember what they are guilty of. This self-blame element is just one of many reasons childhood sexual abuse leads to the erosion of self-esteem.

Emotional control—Finally, children who are coping with childhood sexual abuse maintain tight control over their emotional states. In fact, I believe it entails much more than this. Based on my own experiences, I believe most survivors close down their emotions and mentally separate their mind and body. In essence, I believe they become living shells who go through the motions of being human while feeling dead inside.

One might wonder how it is possible that such deep problems experienced by children are undetected by adults. However, it is essential to remember that the adaptation techniques initially prevented discovery and allowed the child to survive chronic abuse. In fact, to the untrained eye, abused children appear "normal."

* * * * *

Adult survivors use many of the same coping techniques that children employ in enduring their history of abuse. Many adult survivors, myself included, continue to employ these survival techniques as long as they can. When my memories began returning, I was in shock. I tried to suppress the memories. I didn't want to know the horror of my past. I didn't want to feel the pain. This is a natural, self-preserving reaction. However, I was unable to continue to block the memories when it was time for them to return.

As an adult who was just beginning to cope with my abuse history, I used both the altering technique and self-blame in order to deny the severity of what had happened to me. Several years into recovery, I was able to appropriately place the responsibility on my attacker.

However, I still use the psychological altering technique as I assimilate each new, horrible memory. Over the years, as I grew stronger and more able to accept my abuse history, my subconscious slowly lifted the veils that covered the truth, removing them one layer at a time. Only recently have I discarded the last layer and come face to face with the reality of how fully my abuse history has impacted my life and the lives of those close to me.

Years into recovery, I am just beginning to come to terms with the full extent of the emotional control I exercised over myself—not allowing myself to form strong psychological or emotional bonds, not being able to trust myself or others, and not permitting myself to feel physical pain. This technique ensured my survival as a child, but I am convinced that continued implementation in adulthood hampered my ability to heal.

Dissociation

Since so many adults and children employ dissociation as a survival tool, only to later retrieve their memories of abuse, and since it is hard for those who have not experienced severe trauma to understand how memories can be repressed, it seems important to further explore this technique.

Dr. Judith Herman addressed the issue of the commonality of dissociation among abuse survivors by drawing upon three recent studies, involving over 1,000 subjects. "All three studies describe varying degrees of amnesia in subjects who report childhood abuse; the range is from 59 to 78% of the subjects." Further, Dr. Herman asserted that in these studies, "... the degree of amnesia was significantly correlated with the victim's age at the time of the abuse and the degree of violence inflicted." *(Herman, pages 3-4)*

Linda Meyer Williams, Ph.D. conducted research on repression of memories. Her study involved 200 females who reported childhood sexual abuse during the years 1973 through 1975.[2] The victims were treated at the emergency department of a city hospital and forensic evidence was collected. The girls, their family members, and research staff were interviewed shortly after the girls were treated, so there is extensive information available on the actual abuse.

According to Dr. Williams, "The sexual abuse ranged from sexual intercourse (36%) to touching and fondling (33%).... In 14% of the cases, the offender was a member of the immediate family, in 18% he was an extended family member, 29% a friend of the child or of the family, in 30% of the cases a casual acquaintance was involved, and in 22% a stranger. In 21% of the cases, there were multiple perpetrators." *(Williams, page 19)*

In 1990 and 1991 these women were located and interviewed again regarding their memories of the abuse. Dr. Williams' subsequent study, in 1992, is important because it "... provides one of the first opportunities to evaluate whether some women who reported sexual abuse in childhood will fail to disclose the abuse when asked about it seventeen years later." *(Williams, page 19)*

When interviewed, an astounding 38 percent of these women either couldn't recall or chose not to report the abuse. Because the interviews included a wide range of questions asked over a 2-hour period, it is believed the vast majority of this 38 percent truly did not remember. Supporting that conclusion is the fact that over half of these women—53 percent—discussed other childhood sexual abuse experiences. Also, some of the women knew some details of the abuse, but they didn't connect it to themselves.

Williams' study sheds light on three important areas. First, because the women who participated in the study actually reported the abuse to authorities during childhood, it seems reasonable to expect them to be more likely to remember the abuse during their adult years than victims who did not report abuse. Yet, Williams offered, "Thirty-eight percent represents a very large proportion of victimized women who are amnesic for or fail to report their childhood sexual victimization. It suggests that retrospective studies which rely on self-reports of childhood experiences of sexual victimization are likely to result in an underestimation of the true prevalence of such abuse." *(Williams, page 20)*

Secondly, it is highly significant that childhood medical records substantiate the abuse, yet the women couldn't remember. This fact speaks volumes as to the truth of repressed memories.

Thirdly, Williams' study underscores the depth of the psychological trauma inflicted during childhood sexual abuse and the lengths to which child survivors must go to secure their safety. Often the defense mechanisms they develop must remain in place long into the adult years.

Although the recent research into repression of memories doesn't prove all returning memories are real, it does establish that the phenomenon of returning memories is real. In particular, Williams' study indicates a large percentage of victims of sexual abuse repress their memories into the adult years.

Why does dissociation occur? Children who are sexually abused undergo a brutal experience that leaves them feeling fractured, unsafe, and responsible for the attack. Facing the horror may be too difficult.

Many of these children dissociate in order to ensure their continued survival. Further dissociation in adulthood takes place because adult survivors still feel fragmented, their identity scarred during their formative years. They are still fragile. They are still hurting physically, psychologically, emotionally, and spiritually. They still can't cope with the reality that is their past. In order to compensate, they adopt a multitude of coping techniques that can include such destructive behaviors as eating disorders, drug and alcohol abuse, self-mutilation, and sexual promiscuity. The techniques survivors employ assist them in functioning in daily life.

How does dissociation occur? Although the method through which dissociation occurs has not been scientifically proven, it seems reasonable to assume that there are connections between the emotional stress caused by the trauma and resulting biological reactions. Some plausible explanations based on recent trauma studies have been offered. Although this work is still in very early stages, these studies seem to confirm the long-standing clinical observation that traumatic memory is quite different from normal memory. Further study may prove that the two are biologically different.

What makes memories return? Although currently there is no scientific proof that answers this question, I suspect the memories are repressed until survivors are psychologically strong enough to deal with the truth. Then the memories are triggered by something that impacts on survivors' lives: for example, bearing a child; having an abortion; watching a child who is the same age as the survivor was at the time the abuse occurred; surviving another abuse experience; experiencing a flashback during what began as a positive sexual encounter; or (more recently) watching television coverage involving sexual abuse.

In my case, the stage was set during a period of heightened self-esteem and self-discovery connected with writing a diet book. The initial memories were triggered by a sexually intimate setting during which I experienced a flashback.

In his 1993 position paper, Dr. Briere noted, "... access to trauma-relevant information may wax and wane over time as a function of stress, and often can be triggered by environmental events that are especially reminiscent of the original trauma." He further explained, "... therapy which addresses abuse issues also may trigger flashbacks or memories, since the process of treatment almost inherently involves exposure to and processing of traumatic material." *(Briere, page 2)*

In discussing the role of therapy in retrieving memories, Dr. Briere suggested that it is possible for someone to enter therapy with nonexistent or partial memories of childhood trauma, and at some later point to leave therapy with specific memories of abuse. Such an occurrence might appear to an outside observer as evidence that therapy inappropriately created the abuse memories. However, it is important to remember that people seek therapy in order to look at what is not working in their lives.

Dr. Briere also offered, "Part of the recent upsurge of repressed memory reports may ... occur as a result of posttraumatic restimulation events ... through ... increased media coverage of abuse cases in the last several years." *(Briere, page 2)* Thus, exposure to others' histories of abuse may trigger the return of memories.

How can one tell whether or not returning memories are real? In light of the "false" memory controversy, many survivors may hesitate to trust their memories. Therefore, I offer some guidelines on how to determine whether or not the memories are real. In checking their personal histories against the guidelines, those who are retrieving memories should use caution. Basically, I am providing a tool; remember that survivor experiences vary.

These guidelines are not offered as a means of proving or disproving memories or to discourage survivors from believing their memories are real. Nor are they offered to others to be used as a tool in negating survivor memories. My intent is to allow survivors who feel insecure about the truth of their returning memories to try to judge for themselves, to try to remove the doubt and come to a resolve.

Finally, under no circumstances do I wish to negate the idea of returning memories. It is my firm belief that survivors must eventually deal with the reality of their memories if they are going to recover and heal.

Guidelines for Assessing the Truth of Returning Memories

When your memories began returning:
- Did something deep down inside you tell you the memories were real (no matter how much you wanted to disbelieve them)?
- If you didn't have a gut feeling the memories were real, and you then tried to dismiss the memories (or someone else convinced you to disbelieve), did the memories persist? And were more memories revealed later?

  – Did the memories correspond with the unexplained pain you have felt throughout your life? (The pain mentioned here is separate from the new pain you feel now that some memories have been revealed.)
  – Did you "see" the brilliance of the memories (as opposed to observing a dreamlike, cloudy state)?
  – Did your memories return in fragments that often made no sense? As more fragments were revealed to you, did you feel as if you were finally able to begin putting together the pieces of the puzzle that has been your life?
  – Did you feel a strong sense (almost of relief) that at last you were beginning to understand things about your life that you had never been able to put into thoughts or words?
  – If you lived an emotionally isolated life, assuming tremendous responsibility and seeking little support from others, do you now feel you are beginning to understand that isolation?
  – If you were plagued by nightmares, do the returning memories correspond with the images that haunted you?
  – Do your returning memories explain your physical symptoms (e.g., health problems, sexual problems)?
  – Do your returning memories explain your psychological symptoms (e.g., fear, inability to trust or set boundaries; feeling hollow, alone, numb, fractured)?

As time has passed, and you have worked on accepting the memories and your possible history of abuse:

  – Do the facts you know about your life correspond with your returning memories?
  – Do you feel that you are getting physically and emotionally stronger? (This isn't to say that you won't undergo periods of doubt, depression, and poor health; however, over time, survivors who are working toward recovery do get stronger.)
  – Can you name the event(s) that triggered the memories?

As you are able to talk to others about your returning memories:

  – Can you corroborate your memories through the testimony of others?
  – Can you corroborate your memories through physical evidence (e.g., medical records, photographs, locating the place where the abuse occurred)?

– When you think or talk about your memories, do new details suddenly appear that are startling in content and vividness, and yet you get the deep sense they are true? (These are memory validations.)

For those who answered "yes" to a number of the items listed above, the indication is that you should trust your returning memories. You should learn as much as you can about childhood sexual abuse. If you are not in therapy, it would be wise to seek professional help. This process validates your experiences and "normalizes" the craziness you may be feeling. You should also select a method of dealing with your recovery that allows you to chart your progress toward healing. Finally, you should continue to allow the memories to come (without forcing them), slowly work on assimilating them, and try to move forward with your life.

For those who answered "no" to most of the items listed above, particularly if you feel the memories are untrue (as opposed to not wanting them to be true), the indication is that you should continue to question the truth of your memories. This doesn't necessarily mean the memories aren't true. It just means you should move very cautiously in concluding you are a survivor of childhood sexual abuse, and you should seek professional help.

Despite the recent rash of "false" memory charges, therapy provides an appropriate avenue through which survivors may advance their recovery. Dr. Briere described the therapist's role this way, "The clinician should be aware that the process of memory recovery and integration is complex, requires time and support, and should not be rushed or pushed." He further offered, "... interventions which 'inform' the patient of her or his abuse history—despite the patient's protestations to the contrary—are almost never appropriate, nor is the use of any memory recovery technique that capitalizes on suggestion." *(Briere, page 4)*

Those survivors who are already in therapy, but who continue to question the truth of their memories, should carefully evaluate their therapist's methods and experience in the field of childhood sexual abuse. If they feel Briere's parameters are not being observed, it might be advisable to search for a new therapist.

Likewise, therapists whose techniques run counter to these guidelines should consider reevaluating their approach in light of the current controversy.

No matter what results are obtained from following the guidelines on assessing the truth of returning memories, make no mistake about it: survivors' returning memories are real! And only after survivors accept their memories do they begin to feel whole and sane, as if they might be able to recapture their selves.

How should one approach returning memories? Surprisingly, I have found the initial retrieval of memories to be the easiest part, although it was painful. The real work comes with accepting, understanding, going through the stages of recovery, and trying to move beyond the abuse experiences. That journey has proven to be a time-consuming, excruciatingly painful process. But I am convinced there is no other way to attain healing.

Survivors must be cautious and learn to take things one day at a time. They must get used to working with fragments of life knowledge. I didn't force the memories. I didn't want to glimpse the complete picture until it came to me. It was too horrible to reach for, and I didn't want to know until I was psychologically ready to face the whole truth. As each new memory (or series of memories) came to me, the picture became clearer. And after each revelation, I spent time alone, integrating the more recent memories with fragments that were revealed earlier. This time was also spent learning to accept the truth of my past.

In attempting to deal with returning memories, survivors must learn to accept the unacceptable. They must learn to view themselves in an entirely different light. And they must commit to rejecting the negative feelings they have about themselves, to rebuilding themselves from the inside out, to living in a constant state of torment for a lengthy period of time. They must be willing to accept and appreciate small victories while assimilating what appear to be large failures. They must learn to trust themselves. But most of all, they must eventually come to accept that, despite the magnitude of the tragedy that befell them when they were young, nothing compares to the tragedy of not choosing to attempt to recover.

Suggestions for Survivors

- Learn everything you can about childhood sexual abuse.
- Try not to let anyone convince you not to trust your feelings about your past.
- Use the guidelines listed in this chapter if you question the truth of your returning memories.
- After determining that they are real, work on trusting your returning memories; slowly work on accepting your past and assimilating the memories.

- Seek professional help.
- Consider participating in group therapy.
- Find a positive outlet for charting your progress toward recovery.
- Try to remember you are not alone.

Suggestions for Friends and Family of Survivors

- Learn everything you can about childhood sexual abuse.
- Avoid attempting to convince a loved one that the returning memories are not real.
- Gently encourage your loved one to seek professional help.
- Avoid accusing a loved one of lying.
- Avoid applying undue pressure.
- Listen to the survivor and learn how to be supportive.

Conclusion

Many years into my healing journey I am convinced the idea expressed in Misconception #5 is false. There is nothing I could have done to change the way the memories returned, and I believe they came back piece by piece in order to protect my sanity. I suffered excruciating pain with each new memory, and I experienced fear unlike anything I had ever known as the full truth was revealed to me.

Just as I truly believed that I was progressing with my recovery and healing processes, the "false" memory controversy heated up. I was enraged because I realized part of this effort was aimed at silencing survivors—the very people whose testimonies gave me understanding and hope. As I calmed down and investigated the situation, I realized there may be a very small percentage of cases in which abuse charges are false. Those who make such accusations should be encouraged to seek appropriate professional help.

I feel strongly that, after taking so long to find their voices, survivors must not suddenly be silenced by the "false" memory controversy. They owe it to themselves and to the millions of other men, women, and children who were sexually abused to continue to speak out. But, sadly, this controversy will trigger self-doubt, and survivors need to work at maintaining their strength and resolve.

In moving along the healing path, I have gained strength and self-confidence. Today I can accomplish tasks that I couldn't attempt six or even three months ago. I am constantly learning new, positive things about myself while at the same time retrieving additional memories that hinder my recovery. However, no matter how frightening or painful this retrieval process is, it is a key element in recovery because it provides pieces to the puzzle. Pressing ahead is a constant challenge, but one I now know I can meet. I must continue to recover because I cannot continue to lead a compromised life.

"I like living. I have sometimes been wildly, despairingly, acutely miserable, racked with sorrow, but through it all, I still know quite certainly that just to be alive is a grand thing."
— Agatha Christie

"And the day came when the risk it took to remain closed in a bud became more painful than the risk it took to blossom."
— Anais Nin
French/American author

5

Turning Self-Punishment into a Positive Part of Survival

Only through accepting the truth about the past can I end the war that I have waged against myself and my body.

Misconception #6: The child is to blame.

It is easy for people—especially survivors—to believe the child was at fault. After all, why would an adult (especially one whom everyone admires) want to perform sexual activities with children? It is easier to believe that something the child did or said provoked the behavior in the adult. ("She was seductive" is often used as an explanation for what happened—even in cases concerning very young children.) But the child is never responsible for an adult's behavior; adults must always be held accountable for their own actions. It seems simple, but it isn't.

Misconception #6 has a tremendously negative impact on survivors' lives.

* * * * *

Childhood sexual abuse destroys self-esteem and leaves survivors with terrible feelings about themselves and their bodies, even during the repression stage. At 10 (albeit unconsciously), I blamed myself—despite the fact that my attacker was older, stronger, supposedly wiser. To do otherwise would have called into question the safety of the world that surrounded me. At 35, I blamed myself because I thought I should have anticipated his actions. At 46, I take comfort from knowing children shouldn't be expected to protect themselves from an adult's attack, and that I did nothing to invite the horror inflicted upon me.

Men and women survivors feel scarred, branded, ugly. They have extremely poor self-images, and they often direct their rage and hatred (which they may not understand) against themselves. Survivors can exhibit a wide range of self-punishing behaviors that include eating disorders, promiscuity, suicidal tendencies, abuse of drugs and/or alcohol, and entering/enduring destructive relationships.

Often their behavior is an attempt to punish themselves for sins they cannot name. Sometimes the purpose is to alter their abused body. Sometimes it is an attempt to escape the pain, loneliness, and depression that encompasses them.

An even more difficult trait to understand is self-mutilation, which develops more frequently in survivors who were abused at a very young age. Survivors inflict initially minor injuries on themselves. The self-mutilation often continues until survivors, who often feel emotionally and spiritually dead, feel enough physical pain that they can prove to themselves they are alive.

Through this bizarre behavior, survivors are silently crying out to be heard and helped; but because the source of their torment is unknown, often they are rejected. That rejection further supports their negative feelings about themselves.

But the physical aspect of abuse is not the only element to consider; the psychological, emotional, and spiritual pain also runs deep. Based on my experiences, I feel the physical side is, incredibly, the lesser of the two evils. Authors Carol Poston and Karen Lison supported this position in their 1990 book *Reclaiming Our Lives: Hope for Adult Survivors of Incest* when they wrote, "... the scars were not just physical. The worst mutilation was psychological, the one that, like a hot brand on flesh, burned its way into their psyches."[1]

Survivors internally punish themselves through feeling sadness, shame, guilt, and self-hatred; through separating their psyches from their bodies so they can't feel pain; and through being consumed with anger, rage, and fear. They are unable to release these destructive feelings because they believe they are unworthy of anything good. Often they do not understand their feelings and behaviors because they are repressing the memories that would unveil the truth.

Before my memories of being sexually molested began returning, I didn't understand my self-punishing behavior. Over the next 12 years, as I have worked toward recovery and healing, I have found it is very difficult to break the life-long habits that result in further torment and grief. Understanding the cause of my behavior has helped, and I am making progress, but it is an extremely slow and painful process that affects every major aspect of my life.

Before discussing the self-punishment behaviors I attribute to my childhood abuse, I would like to note that the resulting symptoms and illnesses are also exhibited by people who were not sexually abused. For example, in the description that follows, I am not placing value judgments on women who dress in the manner I outline as self-punishing. Dressing in such a manner may actually heighten some women's self-esteem. Each of us is a product of many influences that act upon our belief systems; among them are family, friends, religious teachings, educational system, and cultural setting. Given my background, the manner in which I dressed was provocative; thus, I believed it was bad for me to dress in such a way. Therefore, it was a means through which I punished myself. The same would not hold true for men and women who were raised under different systems and who hold different values.

Also, not every person who is overweight shares my childhood history, nor has everyone who suffers from the health problems I discuss been sexually abused. There are many causes of such problems. Because the units (physical, mental, emotional, spiritual) that make up our "being" result in one system (each complete person), anything (or any action) that attacks one of the units will affect the entire system. This is especially true of an action that destroys one's well-being.

When something so devastating as childhood sexual abuse occurs, it will affect every part of the person. Thus, emotional stress will result in physical stress that will result in the body breaking down (illness). A vicious, destructive, downward spiral begins. That downward spiral can encompass many changes, including the situations described in this chapter.

With the understanding that my belief system was influenced by my environment, the following are some of my self-punishing behaviors.

When I moved out of my parents' home at age 22, I unknowingly prevented further abuse at my attacker's hands. Nevertheless, I felt horrible things about my sexuality and my body. Outside the work setting, whenever my weight was under control, I dressed in a provocative manner—wearing extremely short cutoffs and halter tops, or short dresses with plunging necklines, or see-through blouses. I felt protected by my husband's presence; but, without understanding why, I believed I deserved to be punished. Even though dressing in such a manner made me feel degraded, this self-punishing behavior lasted many years.

During the years just prior to the return of my memories, I drank alcohol almost every night to make the numbness and emptiness disappear. Now that the memories have returned, I seldom drink. I am extremely conscious of the need to work on healing myself rather than escaping my reality through the use of alcohol.

I often over-eat, then feel terrible about myself when I am overweight. For 5 years I controlled my weight, and I felt very good about myself. At that time I was in control of my body and myself, two issues that are very important to survivors. At the present time I am, again, overweight. I know what to do to lose the extra weight; I just have to reach the positive mental state where I can do it!

I felt ugly and often dressed in an unattractive manner. When I am overweight, I hate shopping for new clothes. Like many Americans, I bought into the idea that only those whose bodies are thin deserve to be dressed in an attractive manner. Because I didn't believe I deserved to look nice, I didn't care how I looked, which further damaged my self-image. Finally a friend/colleague told me I would feel better if I tried to look my best, regardless of my weight. Through implementing her advice, I do feel better about myself.

I am extremely uncomfortable in beauty salons. For years, I cut my own hair or had my husband do it. Now I wear it long so I no longer have to worry about it. Recently a friend/colleague purchased some beautiful hair clips for me while she was on vacation. I received so many compliments when wearing them that I experimented with new hairstyles and now enjoy taking care of my hair.

I hated shopping for myself, but I enjoy giving to others things I would like to own. Recently, after voicing such feelings, I realized this was a means of punishing myself. I have always looked upon shopping for myself as a chore, one that must be undertaken only when I need something. I would go to the mall, dart in and buy whatever I needed (without trying it on), take the purchase home, and hope it fit. If it didn't fit, I would deserve the punishment of having to return it.

I learned from a friend/colleague that shopping can be fun! She spent considerable time helping me design a computer system that would fit my current and future writing needs, and then we went computer shopping. We turned the task into a pleasant outing—going to lunch, checking out the computer stores, buying some things for her new house, and then stopping at a department store to buy some accessories for her work clothes. We had so much fun that I realized shopping should not be a chore. I tested the theory by taking a vacation day in the middle of the week (to avoid crowds) and spending four hours at the mall. I took my time, searching for what I liked and trying things on, and purchased several outfits that looked good on me. It was a lesson well learned!

I had been unable to enjoy my body. This began in my early teen years, when I punished myself each week after attending church. I felt I had sinned, but couldn't name my sin. That early trauma ingrained in my psyche so much guilt about physical pleasure—pleasure I didn't feel I deserved—that it has been very difficult for me to break the patterns. And sexual issues have been very hard for me to address. Before my memories returned, intimacy was painful for me because I had tremendous, unexplained fears.

With my husband's encouragement, I learned to experience self-induced pleasure in private moments, but that activity didn't offer the same satisfaction as sharing with my partner. After the memories began returning, I finally understood my sexual problems, but I began experiencing flashbacks during intimacy. This is an extremely difficult issue, one I still haven't completely worked my way through. And I feel tremendous guilt because of what I have put my husband through.

I have been a workaholic all my life. I am currently employed at a university, run my own thesis/dissertation/textbook typing business with my husband, and write in my "free time." My normal pattern for years was to work 14 hours a day and sleep 10, eating while I worked. I was incapable of relaxing and enjoying myself because I didn't believe I deserved any pleasure. When I tried to relax, I felt guilty because I hadn't attended to all the things that needed to be done. The ways in which I dealt with this self-punishing behavior are discussed in the following paragraphs on health issues.

Because I mentally separated my mind from my body, I was unable to feel pain at a conscious level. I suffered through painful headaches and backaches, rubbing the aching body part without really knowing I was in pain. When others brought the condition to my attention, I refused to take medication. Further, I was unable to consciously accept when I was ill because I had declared war on my body. I would suffer through weeks of illness, stubbornly continuing my normal routine, refusing to admit that I was sick and needed help.

My inability to focus on my health led to far worse illnesses. Colds continually developed into bronchitis and led to ear infections. I constantly felt run down.

Five years ago, I began experiencing discomfort while taking my daily run. Although I felt fine when I wasn't running, I kept getting a pain in my right side. I tried rubbing it as I ran, but it didn't go away. I started eating lunch earlier, thinking that my food intake was somehow connected to the problem. But the pain persisted and got worse, so I finally stopped running. Then the pain attacked at night—excruciating back pain that prevented me from standing up straight or breathing properly. Finally, I began having nightly vomiting attacks that lasted from 11:00 p.m. until 4:00 a.m. Sometimes I feared the lining of my stomach was coming out, and I was frightened.

Because I was mentally divorced from my body, I unintentionally provided some false information about my recent medical history when answering the nurse practitioner's questions. But after undergoing a battery of tests, the illness was diagnosed. If I had been conscious of what was happening to my body earlier, the problem would have been treatable. By the time I sought help, it had developed into a life-threatening situation and surgery was the only option.

While recuperating from surgery, I refused to take medication until I was in excruciating pain and, even then, I took morphine only once after I returned home (I chose to use over-the-counter medicine instead). I hated being forced to do nothing but lie around and watch television. I went back to work in two weeks instead of six and paid a dear price by experiencing a slow recovery. I pushed and pushed my body, impeding my progress.

At last I reached the point where my body just couldn't do what I demanded of it. Forced to spend every evening resting, I finally had to accept the limitations. Then I took a hard look at the punishment I had inflicted upon my body over the years, and I realized it didn't deserve such terrible treatment! I learned to accept that my body needed daily rest (apart from sleeping at night), to divorce myself from feeling guilty if I spent a few hours watching television, to actually accept that it is okay for me to relax.

In the more than 20 years I have held my current job, I had never taken a vacation. I utilized vacation time by working reduced hours during the summer in order to complete writing projects. And even that practice was discontinued after surgery. As time passed, my work habits took an enormous mental and physical toll. As my health grew worse, my office staff was reduced due to state economic problems. I knew it was impossible to continue "business as usual" but I felt responsible for everything that happened in the office.

There were no longer enough hours in the day to accomplish what had to be done, and I stopped doing the two things that had served to release my stress—exercising and writing. After four months of putting in a superhuman effort to accomplish the work of two people, I began suffering from burnout.

In the middle of an academic quarter when I knew I was needed at work, I asked for a week off. This was a giant step for me to take. Finally, I realized I am worth taking care of, I am important, my needs are important, my health is important. I am of value! I recognized that my body was hurting, so I visited a doctor without being nagged to go, learned how serious the situation was, and began taking steps to build up my immune system and ensure the return of my health.

One of the worst self-punishing behaviors I have experienced is the inability to feel worthy of acceptance, praise, respect, and love. This creates the constant striving for perfection and high goals. Survivors believe they are what they do. That describes my life. Survivors can't take pleasure from their accomplishments because they feel they do not deserve praise. As each goal is reached, they turn their attention to the next task because they are unable to bask in the warmth of a job well done. Such feelings prevent survivors from expecting or accepting the good wishes of others.

Since survivors feel they are undeserving of affection, they do not strive for the best for themselves. Instead, they strive for the best for others. Survivors need to change this pattern. Their negative self-images can be partially negated by trying to see themselves as others see them. In particular, survivors need to pay close attention to comments made by those whom they have confided in. They need to learn to accept compliments, and to value and bathe themselves in the warmth of the positive things people say about them. Others' observations can also help survivors chart their progress.

Like many survivors, I punished myself by not nurturing myself. Through the support and understanding I have received from my husband, family, and friends, I am slowly turning this behavior around. I am learning to accept that I have value. As my self-esteem has grown, I have begun to take care of myself. And I am learning to slow down!

Survivors need to learn to treat themselves kindly and to pamper themselves. They need to become familiar with their body and try to get on comfortable terms with it. A mirror can serve as an aid in learning to know the body. Survivors could also purchase intimate items that help them feel good about themselves. For women, this might be pretty underwear, a silk nightgown, an exotic perfume. For men, it might be a velour robe, a silk shirt, a special after-shave.

Survivors might buy flowers on a regular basis and invest in tapes of music that put them in the perfect mood to change their negative image of themselves. Women might want to indulge in bubble baths, while both men and women could enjoy sessions with a physical therapist to help relieve the tension in their bodies. Survivors should learn to participate in all types of enjoyable behavior that make them feel special.

Visualization is fun and relaxing. Survivors could close their eyes and picture a peaceful setting they love, possibly a bank by a river or wildflowers in bloom in a meadow. Or they could picture a scene where they are holding themselves lovingly by the hand, just as they would hold the hand of a small child. They should take time to get to know themselves and allow their feelings to come forth.

Tied in with my inability to feel worthy of others' good wishes was my inability to recognize my accomplishments and celebrate my victories. When survivors begin the recovery journey, they are attempting to overcome such a massive problem that their efforts have to be implemented in stages. They should focus on how far they have come, not on how far they have to go. They should remember each step attained is a victory and should be celebrated. It is often hard for survivors to recognize their victories, especially at the beginning of recovery, but they should make the effort!

One way survivors can measure progress is by examining their healing tool. I regularly write about my healing experiences as a means of exploring where I've been and where I am now. This allows me to measure my growth. Recently I've begun including some of my support network friends in the celebration of my victories. I find that I gain even more satisfaction when I include those who have helped me reach this stage in recovery.

Survivors should choose a form of celebration that is non-destructive but brings a great deal of pleasure. They could reward themselves by spending an evening doing something they enjoy (like going to a movie or a play) or buying a book they want to read. During the process, they should remind themselves of the victory they are celebrating. Acknowledging even the small victories along the path toward healing will make up for the fact that complete recovery may be a long way off.

Like many survivors, I punished myself by measuring myself against others. Survivors need to bear in mind that achieving goals may be easier for those who are not attempting to heal from such a devastating experience as childhood sexual abuse. Measuring themselves against others is unfair. It is equally unfair to measure survivors' sometimes bizarre behavior against what is considered to be "normal." Survivors should work toward accepting themselves without applying the standards accepted by society. They need to learn to measure themselves against their past behavior and to accept that even behaving in a manner that is "normal" for them will not always be possible at a particular place and time in their healing.

A common trait among survivors is a narrowing of their world as they retreat into themselves. Although this is a self-protective device, it is also a means of self-punishment. Possibly because of the number of years I was terrorized by my attacker, I severed the mental and physical elements of my being, repressed the memories of my abuse, was unable to form trusting relationships, and refused to participate in many activities. For years after my memories returned, my life consisted of going only to work and the grocery store (accompanied by my husband), taking drives with my husband (but staying in the car), or remaining at home. I felt unsafe in any environment where I was exposed to strangers.

After 12 years of recovery, I am now working on this self-induced isolation and dependency upon my husband. But it is hard. I am moving slowly, taking a step at a time. I now venture out alone in daylight, during the week days, when I will encounter fewer people and, thus, feel safe. I still refuse to go out at night, even with my husband or friends. This deep fear is something that those who were not abused may have trouble understanding. It is a crippling fear, one that colors the lives of those it touches.

Finally, like many survivors, I punished myself by not forgiving myself for what happened to me. This self-punishing behavior is the key to all the destructive behaviors discussed in this chapter. By not forgiving myself, I blamed myself. In blaming myself, I acted in ways that harmed me physically, psychologically, emotionally, and spiritually. And by doing so, I discounted my strengths and goodness and believed I was unworthy of receiving positive feedback, acceptance, and love.

This is the very essence of the downward spiral that survivors must combat from the moment the abuse took place, whether or not they are repressing the memories. In order to pull away from the self-destructive behavior, survivors must release the blame and forgive themselves. This isn't easy, but it is an essential beginning.

Forgiveness is a major issue—and a complicated one. Some people say it is important for survivors to forgive their attacker. However, after years of thinking about this issue, I have concluded it is far more important for survivors to forgive themselves. Survivors were not to blame, but they accepted blame. They may have done things that were inappropriate, or that they felt were wicked; or they may have harbored destructive feelings or wishes. But their actions and thoughts were spawned by events that were beyond their control.

They need to forgive themselves so they can feel everything that is inside them. Forgiving themselves allows them to learn to love themselves. Only then will they be able to heal.

And what about forgiving the attacker? Survivors punish themselves when they are unable to forgive their abusers. Those who were not abused also expect survivors to forgive—sometimes it is demanded. But no one who is not a survivor of childhood sexual abuse can understand a survivor's feelings or history. Others have no right to demand this of survivors! It is wasted effort, and it can harm the survivor.

I am not concerned about my attacker; I am concerned about me. All the rage I feel is because of his actions, not mine. My effort needs to be spent on making me well, not worrying about him. If I can get over my pain, then maybe I will one day be able to forgive him. If so, fine; if not, that's okay, too.

Male survivors who were abused by women may have trouble accepting that a woman's actions could have such far-reaching effects when they are physically stronger than most women. However, they should not discount the damage inflicted upon them just because their abuser was a woman, a member of the "weaker sex." It is important for male survivors to allow themselves to feel the same anger I feel toward my attacker. It may be easier for men to express their anger if they remember the initial damage occurred when they were children. The adult male's mental image of boys is often one of "little men." It may help these survivors to observe boys who are the same age (and approximate size) they were when the abuse took place. I suspect they will be amazed at how innocent and fragile boys are, and how completely helpless they would be if placed at the physical mercy of an adult—be that adult male or female! Perhaps male survivors can then begin to forgive themselves for what happened to them when they were young.

In discussing her unwillingness to bend to the directive "you must forgive to be fully recovered," therapist and incest survivor Barrie Ann Mason wrote, "Most of my adult life has been spent recovering from my childhood. I have a right to be angry ... until I get to the end of the anger. I don't want to hear someone telling me not to be angry, to forgive before I am ready." [2]

Her words accurately express my feelings. Those who say "forgive and forget" don't understand. Even if forgiving my attacker happens at some future point, there is no possibility of ever forgetting. Maybe that's why it is so hard for me to forgive him. His actions have and always will affect my life!

Suggestions for Survivors

- Try to understand you were not to blame.
- Try to understand that childhood sexual abuse is terribly destructive.
- Try to accept that you are a good person.
- Learn to listen to your body.
- Try to accept that pain resulting from childhood sexual abuse is not just physical—there is also psychological, emotional, and spiritual pain.
- Try to recognize ways in which you punish yourself, then work on eliminating those self-destructive behaviors.
- If you are facing drug/substance abuse issues, seek professional help from a therapist with a dual expertise in this area as well as sexual abuse.
- Try to recognize the ways in which you are improving, and reward yourself for each victory (no matter how small).
- Learn to listen to the positive comments made by others and accept their praise.
- Try not to measure yourself against others.
- Learn to be kind to yourself.
- Forgive yourself.
- Learn to think of yourself not as a victim but as a survivor.

Suggestions for Friends and Family of Survivors

- Try to understand that survivors are not to blame.
- Watch for signs that the survivor's health is at risk, and offer gentle reminders that they take care of themselves.
- Try to understand how destructive childhood sexual abuse is.
- Try to understand that childhood sexual abuse can have a negative impact on many aspects of survivors' lives.
- Learn everything possible about childhood sexual abuse to better understand what survivors feel and experience.
- Try to accept that sexual abuse affects all parts of the human organism, not just the physical element.
- Learn to recognize ways in which survivors punish themselves and gently try to negate this harmful behavior.
- Offer encouragement and praise to survivors.

Conclusion

Because of the health problems I have experienced, especially after going through major surgery, I have learned my physical limitations. And I now understand how I punished my self by punishing my body. I have learned to listen to my body. I now rest when my body requires it and take time off from work when I need a break. When I begin experiencing symptoms of illness, I deal with them rather than waiting for the disease to escalate, and I seek medical help when it is warranted. And finally I am able to implement change.

But none of the above would have been possible without negating the idea contained in Misconception #6. Before any true work can be done on recovery and healing, survivors must believe they were not to blame. And then they must look at themselves and identify their self-punishing behaviors. Recognizing negative behavior patterns is the first step toward changing them, just as seeing the barriers survivors erect is the first step toward knocking them down.

My life pattern has always been to venture out into the world in the company of a protector—my husband, a close friend, a group of friends. They always provided a buffer against the world, a cushion that protected me from the things I feared—whether or not they realized they were performing this service. I am now trying to rely on myself. When I recently took a week off work, I spent each morning writing, then I set out on my own. Twice I went shopping; I didn't buy anything, but I enjoyed looking. Three times I went to the movies—alone! I was pleasantly surprised to discover it wasn't a lonely experience. In fact, I enjoyed being by myself. I relaxed and had fun.

During that week, I took another step toward understanding the lessons every survivor must master during recovery. Strengthening my acceptance of myself, I gained new confidence. Through listening to the messages those closest to me have been communicating, I am becoming kinder to myself. And I am beginning to make changes in my life that demonstrate my growing belief that I am worthy of respect. I *do* deserve to be loved.

> *"The only aspect of sexual abuse that survivors are responsible for is healing it."*
> – Margot Silk Forrest, survivor
> Editor of *The Healing Woman*

> *"Those who sit in the grief house will eventually sit in the garden."*
> – Din Hafez
> *The Tongue of the Invisible*

6

Understanding My
Tormented Soul

*Time and again childhood sexual abuse challenges the
meanings of the words in our language. The accepted
definitions of "loneliness" and "pain" don't even
begin to describe my experiences.*

Misconception #7: If the attacker didn't penetrate—i.e., rape—the
child, then he or she wasn't *really* hurt.

Some people do believe rape is the only true form of sexual abuse.
If penetration doesn't occur, many men minimize and discount their
actions by saying, "I only fondled her!" The same argument could be
used by female perpetrators who fail in their attempts to force male
children to have intercourse. However, the pain inflicted by any form
of childhood sexual abuse can come out in bizarre, often unexplain-
able behaviors.

* * * * *

I used to live in a mysterious world. I felt out of sync with those
around me, and I viewed my life as being a puzzle. Often I displayed
bizarre behavior—appearing confident one moment and paralyzed
the next; being aggressive and outgoing at work, yet being totally
inept in social settings; taking on monumental tasks and succeeding,
yet feeling insecure and displaying low self-esteem.

That was the world I lived in until the memories of being sexually
abused returned. When I confided in people close to me, some of them

discounted what happened to me. I doubted myself until a friend who was raped by a trusted family friend when she was a child told me the abuse I experienced was as bad as what she went through. We both knew the terror of possible recurrence and the threat of death. Through her display of compassion, I learned it is unnecessary to compare abuse experiences—they are all destructive.

The pieces of my puzzle slowly fit into place over the last 12 years. As I have walked along the path toward recovery, so much that was a mystery about my life is now explained.

One particular behavior puzzled me for years. I was raised in the Presbyterian faith and I thoroughly accepted those religious teachings. I attended regular church services with my family and tried to practice my faith in my daily life. Although nothing about my observable personality forewarned it, all this changed—dramatically—in my early teens.

I began to feel dirty and unworthy of anything good; I began to feel undeserving of love. The worst time was when we returned home after Sunday church services. I didn't understand why, but I felt guilty. I felt I had no right to be in church and that I was a terrible sinner, but I couldn't name my sin. I felt cheap, like a whore. At those times, I would pick up the entertainment section of the Sunday paper and retreat to my bedroom.

Hating myself, I turned to the pages that advertised X-rated movies—the ones that displayed pictures of large-breasted, scantily clad women. I pretended I was one of them, the best one, the one all men desire. I pretended I had gone to church to cleanse myself, but it didn't work because I hadn't silently confessed my sin. I believed I didn't belong in church because I was such a bad girl. I masturbated to those pictures and then cried because of the horrible way I felt.

As I cried, I prayed to God, asking Him to keep me from repeating the ritual the following Sunday. And I dreaded the arrival of the next weekend because I knew the process would repeat itself, no matter how good I was during the week or how much I prayed for help. I felt it was out of my control, and nothing I could do would make it stop.

The Sunday masturbating sessions didn't end when I threw myself into church activities. They didn't end even when I almost got caught by my mother. Nothing stopped the self-punishing, degrading, uncontrollable habit that tormented me.

When I moved out of my parents' house at age 22, I assessed the situation. I saw that these weekly sessions weren't about enjoying my body, or feeling good about myself, or taking pleasure in my sexuality.

They were about guilt, punishment, and self-loathing. They were destructive, and I knew they must end.

Although I didn't understand what was causing my behavior, I did know it was somehow connected to going to church. Therefore, I reasoned, I must stop going. I did so, and immediately the masturbating sessions ended.

It wasn't until years later, when I recovered the memories of being sexually abused as a child, that I finally understood. At last I knew I had been punishing myself for something that was buried deep in my subconscious. I felt responsible for that man's attack. I felt I deserved what he did to me. I felt the shame and the blame rested with me, even though I didn't remember what had happened. I felt dirty. Each time I went to church, I was unable to cleanse myself because I hadn't admitted my guilt. Therefore, I was an unrepentant sinner parading as one who had not sinned. Since no one else undertook the task of punishing me, I took it upon myself!

My reaction is not unusual for survivors of childhood sexual abuse. They feel they are evil, and they often use vulgar words to describe themselves. Many are caught between needing to turn to God because they believe no one else can understand and fearing the church because of their terrible feelings about themselves.

It took me a long time to accept that I was abused even though my attacker didn't rape me. And I ignored the terror experienced over the next 12 years when he continuously tormented me. I dismissed the fear, the betrayal of trust, the emotional savaging of my well-being.

It wasn't until 9 years into my recovery process that I retrieved memories that allowed me to understand the true source of my fear—his death threats. All survivors, no matter what form the physical assault against them took, suffer from some form of emotional trauma. All survivors who wish to recover must deal with the destruction resulting from the abuse. All survivors experience similar, seemingly unreasonable fears surrounding security and safety issues.

However, once survivors accept that they were not to blame, that nothing they could have done would have prevented the abuse, they can release the shame. In order to do this, they must learn that they are not alone.

Suggestions for Survivors

- Try to accept that childhood sexual abuse has far-reaching effects and may have resulted in bizarre behavior that you don't understand.

- Try to understand how you have blamed and punished yourself, even if you were repressing the memories.
- Try to accept that you weren't responsible for what happened.
- Try to release the blame.
- Try to release the shame.
- Learn to think of yourself as a survivor rather than a victim.

Suggestions for Friends and Family of Survivors

- Try to accept that childhood sexual abuse will color many aspects of survivors' lives.
- Try not to blame survivors.
- Try to believe that survivors could not have prevented the abuse.
- Try to understand that survivors didn't want these horrible things to happen to them.
- Try to help survivors release the shame of having been abused through acceptance and supportive efforts.

Conclusion

As the example discussed in this chapter illustrates, childhood sexual abuse colors many aspects of survivors' lives. Sadly, often survivors don't understand the far-reaching effect their history of abuse has on their lives. Because they don't understand the reason behind their actions, they are often confused and afraid, and display strange behaviors. They feel ashamed. After I was finally able to accept what happened and that it was not my fault, I forgave myself.

As I have worked toward recovery, I have grown on so many levels. But I still have not been able to return to church. Perhaps fear keeps me from attending—fear that going back will again trigger the behavior with which I punished myself for almost 10 years. Or perhaps I no longer feel the need for organized religion because I never abandoned the deep, inner faith that has carried me through all the dark days of torment and discovery.

At times I miss the beauty of the ritual of organized religion, especially the music. But whenever I feel the need to, I sing hymns.

"You can't turn off the darkness, but you can turn on the light."
– Old saying

"We are healed by what we turn toward, not what we turn from."
– Anonymous

7

Understanding My Inconsistencies

For survivors of childhood sexual abuse, the demons reside within as well as without. Although we may eventually escape the outer demons (our abusers), we can't escape the inner demons until we face the truth.

Misconception #8: Once survivors reach the point of controlling their emotions, they are all right; they should then begin to put the past behind them and get on with their lives.

Actually, survivors have been controlling themselves all their lives—repressing, then denying. As the experiences described in this chapter demonstrate, only when survivors finally release their emotions and uncork all the bottled-up hurt, pain, and anguish, can they begin to heal.

* * * * *

From my early teen years until I was 34 years old, I felt as if a stranger occupied my body. I was not afraid of this stranger, but I was puzzled by her presence. She made decisions that often confused me, but I never questioned her choices. I allowed her to guide me because I felt she protected me from some dark secret that could destroy me.

During those years, I thought of my life as fragmented, a puzzle, clouded by dark shadows, often spinning out of my control. I would have described myself as being splintered, empty, hollow, confused, drained, anxious, crazy, afraid, tormented. And yet everyone around me would have described me as happy and normal. My behavior was consciously and unconsciously designed to cloak the truth and protect the secret from discovery.

And then I began recovering my memories of being sexually abused, and I started to understand.

Survivors of childhood sexual abuse exhibit conflicting behaviors that confuse themselves as well as the people close to them. They experience numerous feelings that are in conflict with the picture they present to the world of a whole person. Physical/body issues are usually very difficult for them to confront. They also suffer from a wide array of physical symptoms and ailments that are directly related to their childhood trauma.

It is my hope that discussing my idiosyncrasies, feelings, physical/body issues, and physical symptoms will help other survivors come to terms with their torment as they begin to understand the world survivors occupy. Further, I hope, through reading my story, men and women survivors who are still repressing or denying the truth of their past will find the strength to face themselves and make the commitment to recover. Choosing to heal is the best decision I have ever made!

Idiosyncrasies

The following are some of the idiosyncrasies that are a part of my life.

- Beginning in my early teen years I felt my life was a fragmented puzzle, yet I have achieved most of my goals.
- In high school and college, I sat on the sidelines at social gatherings (or chose not to attend), too shy to participate, while at the same time I was a student leader.
- I couldn't walk alone across a crowded restaurant to get to a restroom, and yet I won several scholarships in college and traveled around the world.
- Even though I was involved in a long-term relationship in college, a male friend described me as "asexual."
- At times I am so insecure that I can't pick up the telephone to call our gardener, yet I manage a very busy academic office.
- Some days it saps my energy just to get out of bed or cross a street, yet I am the leader of several staff groups at work.
- I am aggressive and competent, while at the same time I am anxious and insecure.

- I swing from being totally dependent to being fiercely independent, depending on the circumstances that surround me.
- One moment I feel confident, like there is nothing I can't do, and the next moment I feel paralyzed.
- When I succeed in performing monumental tasks, I take little pride in my accomplishments.
- Often I feel lonely, although I am blessed with a circle of close friends.
- At times I must speak in front of large groups, but on a bad day I have difficulty going to the grocery store alone.
- Although I love children, I agonized and then consciously decided not to have children of my own.

Feelings

These are some of the feelings that have tormented me.
- I felt old, self-sufficient, responsible for myself even during my early teens. I was a "parentified child," bearing the burden of protecting myself and my mother from the threats of my attacker. Eventually I felt responsible for the safety and well-being of my entire family. Because of my attacker's actions, I had ceased to feel young and innocent.
- From my early teen years, I was tormented each time I went to church—feeling I was a wicked girl and yet not being able to name my sin.
- I didn't know what security and trust were.
- I felt insecure and suffered from low self-esteem.
- Before the memories returned, and even years into recovery, I was unable to feel anything but deep pain. Once a high school friend wanted me to do something and I declined. She grabbed my wrists and dug her long fingernails into my skin. I refused to give in and didn't feel the pain until her nails had gouged deep into my flesh. I still bear the scars on one wrist.
- I felt unworthy of acceptance, praise, and love.
- I felt responsible for things that were not my fault. I believed I deserved to be blamed.
- I constantly felt that my deeds were the true picture of my self, that they replaced me.
- I continuously set high goals for myself in order to prove my value as a human being.
- Often I feel totally out of sync with the world around me.

- I fear men, and it takes a great deal of patience and time before any male can gain my trust.
- I denied wanting to fall in love and emphatically asserted I would never marry. I felt I could not enter a permanent relationship that required trusting a man.
- At times I am consumed with a deep sadness (depression) that permeates my whole being.
- Often I feel like crying for no reason (when I do cry, frequently it is hard to stop).
- At times I am consumed with such anger that I am overwhelmed. It sometimes comes out in unwarranted verbal attacks on my husband or is directed at male colleagues who occasionally treat me as if they have power over me.
- Often I feel out of control; yet I feel a tremendous need to be in control.

Physical/Body Issues

Adding to the torment I felt, because of the conflicting emotions that raged through my body, were the problems I had to deal with concerning physical/body issues.

- I felt as if my body were not a part of me.
- During high school and college, I had a difficult time discussing or writing about sexual issues or exploring romantic relationships in literature classes.
- I had trouble watching people (including my parents) display physical signs of affection.
- I didn't want to be touched.
- I gained no pleasure from myself or my body.
- I felt ugly.
- I have always been sexually repressed. This constantly presented a problem in forming close relationships with men, particularly since my early adult years occurred during the "sexual revolution."
- I have had several paranormal experiences, including one visitation from the dead and three out-of-body experiences (none self-induced). These experiences have helped me deal with the knowledge of the pain that was inflicted on my body. They have also helped me understand the world we live in and the world we enter after this life ceases. I have learned not to be afraid of this type of "unknown."

- Often I experience unexplained fear and I feel like a trapped animal.
- I need to be safe. I feel most safe when I am home or at work. Most of the time I choose to go nowhere else.

Physical Symptoms

Finally, I have experienced the following physical symptoms and ailments that I feel are directly related to my childhood trauma.

- I felt like there was a hole inside me, and that it sapped my energy and slowly drained off my life force.
- I have displayed the following (often pain-inducing) behaviors: rocking back and forth; twisting, sucking, chewing, pulling hard on my hair; picking at scabs; chewing my nails and tearing my cuticles until they bled and became infected; digging my fingernails into the palms of my hands; clenching my jaw and grinding my teeth; biting on my arm so hard it left deep teethmarks; sucking on my arm until blood gathered under my skin; pinching myself so hard I bruised; inserting sharp pins or blades into my flesh. When the pain finally reached my conscious mind, I felt better because the numbness had disappeared and at last I knew I could feel.
- I have trouble getting to sleep. When I finally fall asleep, often I suffer from nightmares—particularly when new, traumatic memories appear.
- I was unable to use tampons until after I married and had intercourse. Even now, I frequently have difficulty inserting them.
- In recent years, I have used a panty liner at all times. This has created some gynecological problems related to not getting enough air circulation, and I am currently trying to break this habit. This is not an uncommon trait in female survivors, and it results from feeling unclean. I have heard of female survivors who wear tampons at all times, resulting in worse problems than those I experience.
- I regularly suffered from vaginal infections. For a period of 2 years, during the time just prior to and directly after the initial recovery of my memories, I experienced them about every 6 weeks.
- I have had urinary tract infections, a uterine fibroid tumor, and suffer from terrible premenstrual syndrome (PMS).

- I suffer from terrible headaches that don't respond to medication. Often these headaches last several days.
- My stomach problems escalated to the point that when I finally was conscious of my pain, I required surgery. Since surgery, I still have an extremely sensitive stomach that responds with intense pain to the wrong foods and stress.
- During my childhood, adolescent, and early adult years, I suffered from constipation. Throughout my mid-adult years, I have suffered from intermittent diarrhea.
- I have experienced cramping symptoms from my adolescent years to the present time.
- I suffer from excruciating lower back pain and pain at the back of my neck.
- Often I am in pain but I do not feel it. I become aware of the pain when others ask why I am rubbing my back, neck, or forehead. When I met with my surgeon prior to surgery, she said I must have been in terrible pain for several years. If I had sought medical intervention earlier, the problem could have been treated without surgery. I sought help the moment I became aware of the pain.
- During my adult years, I have constantly fought against colds, flu, sore throats, middle and inner ear infections, and bronchitis. For long periods of time, my immune system has been ineffective in fighting disease.
- I suffer from fatigue, despite sleeping long hours.
- I suffer from nervousness when there appears to be no reason for it.
- I suffer from a series of allergies, the first of which dates back to my late teens. As I have poured energy into my recovery work, my allergies have gotten progressively worse and new ones have developed. The more recent allergies include: such sensitive skin that I regularly get poison oak without going anywhere near plants, constant outer ear infections, recurring rashes on my face, neck, and one arm. Using medications relieves the symptoms only temporarily (and for very brief periods of time) at best.
- I frequently have difficulty breathing. The symptoms include feeling like I can't get enough air because someone is applying pressure to my chest and feeling like someone is blocking my mouth and nostrils.
- I regularly experience hot flashes. Medical tests indicate they are not connected with the pre-menopausal condition.

- I break out in icy chills and experience night sweats.
- I have waged a life-long weight battle. The only extended period of time in my life when I was not overweight was a 5-year period just before and after my memories began returning. Over-eating is a form of self-punishment; it is also one way in which I make myself unattractive to men.
- Because I can't relax, I experience physical pain during sexual intercourse. Like many survivors, since my memories have returned I suffer from flashbacks during moments of intimacy.

I realize the inconsistencies discussed in this chapter, especially the low self-esteem, health, and weight problems, are also found in those who did not experience childhood sexual abuse. As I mentioned in Chapter 5, "Turning Self-Punishment Into a Positive Part of Survival," there are many reasons for these types of problems. (Outside stressors such as work conflicts, relationship problems, and financial difficulties can also lead to individuals not taking care of themselves.)

However, these types of problems are found throughout the research on survivors of childhood sexual abuse. Although people who were not abused may suffer from a few of these symptoms, the indications suggest that both male and female survivors suffer from a wide range of symptoms.

Further, the symptoms may be so prevalent in survivors because we frequently cut ourselves off from our bodies in order not to feel the pain of our past. Unfortunately, that protective device also cuts us off from the pain of our present. Our symptoms and illnesses become worse because we are not aware of them; thus, we do not treat them in the beginning stages.

In determining whether or not my theories are supported by research in the field, I contacted Vincent J. Felitti, M.D., who is associated with the Kaiser Permanente Medical Care Program in San Diego, California. [1] He has been doing research related to chronic illness and childhood sexual abuse for several years.

One of his studies involved examining complete medical records of 131 adult members of one of America's major health maintenance organizations (HMO). These patients were examined decades after their childhood sexual abuse experiences (incest, molestation, and/or rape), which makes this follow-up investigation unique and extremely important. The study was prompted by the observation that a large number of patients who failed a weight control program revealed a history of childhood sexual abuse and also displayed a pattern of medical symptoms. The patients answered an extensive questionnaire and the study population consisted of a broad range of adults. Patient medical records were reviewed, some going back 25 years.

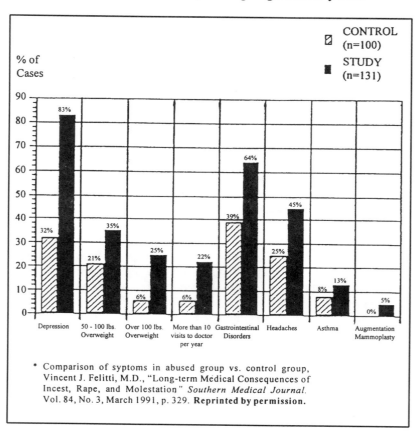

* Comparison of syptoms in abused group vs. control group, Vincent J. Felitti, M.D., "Long-term Medical Consequences of Incest, Rape, and Molestation" *Southern Medical Journal.* Vol. 84, No. 3, March 1991, p. 329. **Reprinted by permission.**

The study, which lasted three months, included experimental and control groups matched for sex and age. Individuals in the experimental group identified themselves as having suffered some form of childhood sexual abuse, while members of the control group did not— either because their histories were free of such abuse or because they were unaware or unwilling to disclose such abuse. These two groups were reviewed for the following symptoms: "... depression, obesity, asthma, allergic rhinitis, smoking, chronic back pain, chronic headaches, recurrent abdominal distress, surgery, augmentation mammoplasty, medical care utilization, and marital stability."*(Felitti-1991, page 328)* The dependent variables were chosen because of the frequency with which they appeared in a preliminary medical chart review.

Dr. Felitti noted, "The subject patients were found to be distinct for chronic depression, morbid obesity, marital instability, high utilization of medical care, and certain psychosomatic symptoms, particularly chronic gastrointestinal distress and recurrent headaches." *(Felitti-1991, page 328)* The results of Dr. Felitti's study astounded me because they closely paralleled my own medical history. Three findings are particularly significant to my case.

First, "The average time between sexual abuse and this evaluation was more than three decades. For more than 90 percent of the patients, this was the first time it had ever been discussed."*(Felitti-1991, page 329)* My abuse began when I was 10, and I have not yet discussed it with any of my doctors.

Second, the figure dramatically shows that, for each symptom, a far greater percentage of sufferers were sexually abused as children.

Third, all the variables correspond with my history except smoking, having an unstable marriage, and augmentation mammoplasty. I do not smoke. Although I would not characterize my marriage as being "unstable," there is no doubt that my history of abuse has dramatically impacted upon my relationship with my husband. If he were not so patient and understanding, there is every reason to believe our marriage would be unstable.

At first I was surprised that augmentation mammoplasty was a variable in the Felitti study, especially since one frequent reason for undergoing breast enlargement surgery (apart from reconstructive surgery following breast cancer) is to enhance physical appearance (presumably to appear more attractive to men). Such an action would be in opposition to my own feelings of wanting to appear unattractive to men. After giving the matter considerable thought, I propose the following five reasons why a survivor might undergo such surgery:

- to change the body so it is no longer like the damaged one;
- to change the breasts so they are not the ones that were touched by their attacker;
- to repair the badly damaged body image;
- to enhance self-esteem;
- to further implement self-tormenting behavior.

These reasons seem to fit the psychological makeup of women survivors. I am sure other survivors could add to this list.

Among the conclusions drawn from Dr. Felitti's 1991 study are the following:

- Depression (which previously had been reported for only a few years after abuse) actually lasts decades after the abuse.
- Depression is associated with obesity; obesity is correlated with the history of abuse.
- There is a connection between chronic psychosomatic symptoms (e.g., recurrent headaches, gastrointestinal distress) and childhood sexual abuse. This connection had previously been uncovered in psychiatric settings; Dr. Felitti discovered the same connection in the general medical population.
- Patients with a history of sexual abuse often are high users of medical care.
- Many of these patients have a history of multiple categories of sexual abuse (e.g., incest and rape) at the hands of multiple abusers.
- Marital instability is one result of childhood sexual abuse.

After making the connection between obesity, depression, and a history of childhood sexual abuse, Dr. Felitti studied obesity in light of a number of chronic stress variables. This second study included 100 obese adults and 100 control adults who had never been overweight. Through interviews, it was learned that "... the obese applicants were found to be different at a highly significant level in the prevalence of childhood sexual abuse, nonsexual childhood abuse, early parental loss, parental alcoholism, chronic depression, and marital family dysfunction in their own adult lives." *(Felitti-1993, page 732)*

The report is based on the original notes of five different interviewers (structured inquiry), the patients' medical records (which often covered decades), notes from secondary interviews, and any additional information provided by the nursing staff. I felt the information obtained relating to the variable of childhood sexual abuse was impressive, especially since it was only one of a number of trauma-related stressors under study.

In Dr. Felitti's 1993 study, 25 percent of the obese group were survivors of childhood sexual abuse. Although only the first episode of sexual abuse was used in determining which category the participant fell into, 29 percent of those who were sexually abused reported additional abuse experiences that would have placed them in multiple categories. Also, one in six of those who were abused reported abuse by multiple perpetrators within their category. Four participants said they couldn't recall whether they had been molested, so they were treated as if they had not been molested. *(Felitti-1993, page 734)*

In contrast, of those in the slender group, only 6 percent reported having been sexually abused as a child. None of these patients was uncertain about their recall of abuse experiences.

In addressing the new information uncovered during this study, Dr. Felitti wrote, "Obese patients applying to our VLCD [Very Low Calorie Diet] program have an unexpectedly high prevalence of previous sexual abuse, chronic depression, and dysfunctional family life. They differ significantly from a control group of adults who have never been overweight." *(Felitti-1993, page 734)* The chart dramatically outlines the differences in these two groups for the specified variables.

Further, information obtained in this study indicates that "... the onset of obesity frequently coincides with identifiable events having significant psychological impact." One of these factors frequently mentioned was childhood sexual abuse. In concluding the report on his study, Dr. Felitti said, "Physicians who seek to understand what is at the core of obesity must pursue a history of depression, physical or sexual abuse, and being part of a dysfunctional family."*(Felitti-1993, pages 735-736)*

Depression, Anxiety, and Substance Abuse in the Obese and Slender Groups

Characteristic	Obese	Slender
Chronic Depression	57%	22%
Chronic Anxiety	27%	15%
Rage Reactions	12%	3%
Chronic Sleep Disturbance	46%	23%
History of Alcohol or Drug Abuse	30%	18%

* Vincent J. Felitti, M.D., "Childhood Sexual Abuse, Depression, and Family Dysfunction in Adult Obese Patients: A Case Control Study," Southern Medical Journal, Vol. 86, No. 7, July 1993, p. 734. **Reprinted by Permission.**

During a telephone interview with me, Dr. Felitti spoke about his current research. He is working with information obtained from

15,000 patients from general medicine who have chosen to complete medical examinations. The questionnaire these patients fill out reveals information about their childhood experiences (including family histories on alcoholism, drug usage, divorce, physical abuse, suicide, committing violent crimes, and sexual abuse). It also solicits extensive information about the patient's personal and medical histories (including questions about sleeping habits and psychological state).

The results of this study will report on the patient's adult health status while taking into consideration each participant's childhood history. This approach attempts to understand the whole patient.

Such an approach would be of tremendous help to my doctors in treating all of my symptoms. At various times I have seen medical doctors, dermatologists, gynecologists, an allergist, nurse practitioners, and a surgeon. None of these professionals knows the truth about my past, yet they have all treated medical problems that stem from my history of abuse. In short, I have allowed them to see the fragments of my body, just as I have treated myself as a fractured person. As I now attempt to reunite my body into one being (recognizing the physical, mental, emotional, and spiritual units are all elements of my self), I must approach my medical treatment in a like manner.

This isn't an easy proposition for survivors because many have spent their entire lives diminishing the extent of the abuse and its affect on them. Only through writing this book have I come face to face with the full truth. The current medical studies that demonstrate the link between childhood sexual abuse and chronic illness offer hope for the millions of men, women, and children who are survivors. Once those in the medical profession are able to discover the cause of survivors' problems and address them as whole people, they will begin to feel whole. And through that process, they will truly begin to heal.

* * * * *

The following example shows how the inconsistencies that are a part of survivors' lives compounded my relationship with my family.

For many years after I moved out of my parents' home, I slept badly the night before I planned to visit them. Often, I had nightmares before these visits. While I was at their house, I experienced a variety of physical discomforts including being nervous, edgy, jumpy; having headaches before and during the visits; and experiencing difficulty breathing. My voice often shook uncontrollably; I was cold and broke out in icy sweats. I felt like I had to urinate every five minutes, and my stomach was so upset that I feared I would vomit.

I always felt like a child when I returned to my parents' home. And I wanted to please them, so I suppressed my opinions and feelings. Whatever the personal cost, I wanted to keep the peace. It was as if I could not be myself while I was around them.

Over the last few years, as I have grown stronger through my recovery, I reached the point where I felt confident enough to express my opinions when with my parents. When appropriate, I disagree with them. I feel we now have a healthier, much more open relationship, and we have some interesting discussions. For the first time in my life, I feel like an adult when I am with them. I no longer experience the negative physical symptoms to the extent I previously did.

However, now that I am much more attuned to my bodily responses, I feel my reactions to a far greater extent. As I drove through their neighborhood before my last few visits, I felt the uneasiness in my stomach. Although I looked forward to seeing them, I was very nervous.

Suddenly I understood the cause of my unrest. Even after so many years have passed, to me, that house is still a threatening environment. It was the location where the last 5 years of terrorization took place. It was the place where my attacker intended to rape me.

During a recent visit, my mother took me upstairs to show me some changes they had made in the house. I felt fine until I walked into the bedroom that had been mine. Twenty-four years have passed since I occupied that space, and my sister moved into the room after I left the house. There was nothing in the room that had been mine. Although it had been painted, refurnished, recarpeted, and redecorated, I was drawn back in time and saw the room as it looked when I occupied it. I relived the last meeting with my attacker. His sinister presence still occupies that room and I suspect, for me, it always will.

Although I don't blame my parents for what happened, I am still afraid of returning to their home—even though my attacker is dead. I wonder if that feeling will ever disappear.

* * * * *

Once my memories began returning, my life seemed like a kaleidoscope where everything was out of my control. Events seemed to be manipulated by others—the colors too bright, the action too fast, the deeds too terrifying to imagine. For a time I fought against knowing the truth, but the memories kept returning and the pieces of my puzzle kept stabbing me until they fit into place. It hurt like hell! But at last I gained strength and decided to face the truth. I knew I had to reclaim and then come to terms with my past if the pieces of my fragmented self were ever going to fit together again.

During this reclaiming process, I took comfort from knowing I was not going insane. At last all the inconsistencies and mysteries that marked my life made sense, and I realized the craziness represented my struggle for survival. With acceptance came the realization that there was nothing I could do to remove the past. My life always has been influenced by the tragedy of my youth, and it always will be.

Despite my decision to recover, my outward attempts to maintain control did not mean I was all right. I still carried the burden of dealing with my torment alone. I have learned recovery and healing are about taking back control of myself and my life. However, regaining control doesn't mean survivors should suppress their emotions. These emotions have been bottled up inside survivors for years, poisoning and preventing them from recovering. They should learn to release them by crying, feeling their sorrow, feeling their anger and rage. Accepting emotions as valid and reasonable is another way for survivors to progress toward recovery.

Although women have been taught since childhood not to express violent feelings like rage, and men have been taught not to express their more vulnerable feelings, survivors must learn it is healthy to release these emotions. They have to deal with how they feel about the abuse. All survivors have to learn to open up, to allow some of the pain to escape, to release the burden.

It's even okay for survivors to release these feelings in front of people they have trusted with their secrets. They shouldn't be embarrassed about crying in front of others. Nor should they be concerned that their tears will never end. When I began recovering the memories of my past, I cried a lot. When I began confiding in others, I had no control over the tears. Sometimes they came in painful sobs that I thought would never stop. But as I began to realize I was not to blame, and as I dealt with the truth, I grew stronger. When my self-esteem improved, I regained control and the tears stopped.

Suggestions for Survivors

- Try to accept your idiosyncrasies and inconsistencies.
- Try to accept that your behavior protected you and ensured your survival during the period of your abuse.
- Try to understand that all sexual abuse experiences are terribly damaging.
- Learn to trust your instincts.
- Learn to listen to your body. This can be accomplished by changing life patterns that result in suppressing feelings, emotions, and the ability to feel pain. It helps to set time aside to be

alone and unoccupied (e.g., meditating). Some additional tools are exercising and developing creative talents (e.g., writing, painting).

- Learn to monitor your health and take steps to protect yourself from illness.
- Learn to accept (and feel worthy of) praise.
- Try not to accept blame for things that are not your fault.
- Work on accepting your body apart from the abuse experiences. This entails retraining and correcting the mental image that rejects the body and denies the beauty and goodness of the physical part of human existence.
- Work on regaining control of your life.
- Try to accept your emotions as valid and reasonable, then work on releasing them.
- Work on changing things that can be changed while accepting the things that cannot be changed.
- Try to accept who you are.
- Learn to think of yourself as a survivor, rather than a victim.

Suggestions for Friends and Family of Survivors

- Try not to assume survivors who appear to be all right necessarily are.
- Try to understand that all sexual abuse experiences are terribly damaging.
- Try to accept survivors' limitations and inconsistencies.
- Try to accept survivors as they are.
- Gently encourage survivors to change in ways they want to change.
- Support survivors' efforts to recover and heal without placing unreasonable expectations on their progress.
- Try to realize the abuse experiences will always be a part of the survivor.
- Try to understand the effort it has taken for victims of childhood sexual abuse to survive.

Conclusion

All the puzzling things that are a part of survivors' lives—the unknowns, the blanks, the shadows, the inconsistencies in their behavior, the unexplained fears, the choices they made that they can't explain, the chronic medical problems—are directly related to their childhood abuse. By repressing the memories and living a life that, to them, seems fragmented, they chose to survive. Even after the memories return, they won't suddenly become like "normal" people. They will still exhibit behaviors that are confusing, and they will still experience a multitude of physical symptoms. They must accept the situation and rejoice that at least now they understand.

Several years after my memories began returning and I made the decision to heal, I strived to learn to control the way the past influences my life rather than allowing it to control me. Adopting this new goal didn't lessen the pain or change the fact that there was still a monumental task ahead of me. I quickly realized there was only one path I could take if my inner self were ever going to match the picture of the whole woman I presented to the world—I had to become acquainted with the beloved stranger who resided within me. Unlocking her knowledge was the key to reclaiming myself.

"You can outdistance that which is running after you, but you cannot outdistance that which is running inside you."
– African proverb

"To the child—and therefore to the inner child at the core of every survivor—even the illusion of control provides some relief."
– Margot Silk Forrest, survivor
Editor of *The Healing Woman*

8

Dreams Lost, Dreams Found

The events from the past beat through me just as blood beats through my body. There isn't a part of my being that hasn't been colored by my history of abuse. It has been an influencing factor on the decisions I have made and the path my life has taken—whether or not I remembered the abuse at the time.

Misconception #9: Childhood sexual abuse is no big deal. Survivors should just forget about it and get on with their lives.

This misconception is based on lack of understanding of what happens when children are abused. Not only are they physically harmed, but they are mentally, emotionally, and spiritually injured as well. Survivors are robbed of so many things—childhood, joy in themselves, ability to excitedly anticipate the growing-up process, trust, self-esteem, ability to set boundaries. The list could be a mile long. In place of these wonderful traits, survivors are left with guilt, dread, self-blame, anxiety, fear, shame! Survivors are so traumatized that in many cases they repress the memories in order to survive the ordeal. As the following personal experience shows, this is not something one can merely forget in order to move ahead with life!

* * * * *

One of the most important and influential people in my life is my father's sister. She was, and is, a commanding person; but to me, she was also daring and exciting. She has lived an extraordinary life. She served in the Army Nurse Corps, darting into my world as her assignments permitted. Her letters kept me informed and her visits were accompanied by color slides and tales of the exotic places she visited. And the gifts she sent or delivered at Christmas and for birthdays were equally intriguing—dolls from around the world; a beautiful, hand-painted, rice-paper Japanese umbrella that was my pride and joy; clothing from other cultures; books whose pictures called to me at a very young age. Her adventures planted in me the desire to travel as well as the need to serve others.

She was my role model and my idol. My childhood dream matched her adult one—when she was ready to retire, I would replace her. As a child, I followed her footsteps; I wanted to walk in her shoes as an adult. It wasn't until I reached adulthood and knew I would never capture that dream that I fully realized how truly remarkable she is, and how proud of her I am. By the time she retired, she held the rank of lieutenant colonel. She served overseas during World War II and the Korean War. Near the end of her distinguished career, she served as the chief nurse at the largest evacuation hospital in South Vietnam.

Although her stint in Vietnam occurred almost 30 years ago, and she tried to make her letters cheerful so as not to worry her family, I distinctly remember some things that she couldn't keep inside—the long hours spent at the operating tables, how young her patients were, her own anguish over the suffering and death. After retirement, she continued to serve by participating in a counseling clinic for Vietnam veterans. She was also one of the leaders of the Vietnam Women's Memorial Project.

Throughout my childhood and young adult life I wanted to be like her. I wanted to take over where she left off and build on her years of service. And yet it was not to be. Although I didn't realize it at the time, my dream was crushed when I was sexually molested. In a matter of minutes, my world changed. I became afraid of all men. I feared for my life and the well-being of my family. And because the attack occurred in my parents' home, I lost my "safe" world.

Repressing the memories was my only means of survival, and yet I clung to my dream. In fact, I gained comfort from picturing myself grown up, living in a foreign country, serving others, healing. Through that dream, I was transported away from the horror that was my reality over the next 12 years as my attacker visited our home and continued to terrorize me.

During my sophomore year in high school, I enrolled in a biology class. This was the first step toward obtaining the education I needed to carry out my dream. In college, I took biology, genetics, psychology, and health classes; but I didn't apply for admission to the nursing program. Without ever making a conscious decision about my future, I released the dream of following in my aunt's footsteps. I felt fragmented and undirected. For the first time, I couldn't answer the question, "What do you want to do with your life?" Somehow, deep inside I knew I would never become an army nurse. But I didn't understand why.

My unvoiced decision unintentionally drove the first of many wedges between us. I felt my aunt's disappointment, and was ashamed because I couldn't explain my choice. Her retirement from the Army Nurse Corps presented a particularly difficult moment because I knew she must be feeling what I was thinking—that I had not kept my part of the bargain. I was tormented because I knew she was not the only one who had lost her dream; I had lost mine.

During my college years, there were several areas I excelled in that held my interest, but I had a difficult time choosing a major. I felt torn because I didn't have a burning desire to pursue another career. At last I made the selection by default. Of the three possible choices—English, music, or sociology—the latter had the least negative requirements. It demanded only 1 year of foreign language and had no public performance requirement. And it contained a positive element the other majors lacked. It offered the chance to serve others.

Once my decision was made, I selected a concentration in social psychology that would allow me to do social work. Eventually my career dream became working with delinquent children. But that plan was derailed after my husband asked, "How are you ever going to relate to such children?" He realized my background and lack of exposure would prevent me from understanding the very kids I wanted to help. Further, he knew, although I could empathize with them, I would internalize their pain and eventually be destroyed by what I saw. And I think, without understanding why, he sensed my need to feel safe and in control; it would have been impossible to achieve these goals in such a career.

After listening to his concerns, I carefully explored my feelings and gave up this second dream, although I completed the university degree. My educational background has served me well by guiding me in performing my duties as a university employee and in helping me cope once my memories of being sexually abused began returning.

Twelve years into my recovery process I finally understand why I was unable to capture my childhood dream. Because of my fear of men generated by the attack against me, I could never have felt safe in a military setting. I would have been one of a few women among hundreds or thousands of men. By unconsciously choosing not to follow that dream, I protected myself. In short, I accepted my limitations without understanding them.

That acceptance is a key to survival for victims of childhood sexual abuse because it allows them to set reasonable goals, a technique they need to master. They shouldn't demand instant or complete recovery or set goals that are impossible to reach. Asking too much of themselves, especially at the beginning stages of recovery, could set them up for failure and might result in further damage to their self-esteem and confidence. Initially, they should set small goals that can easily be reached. Then they can set larger goals as they grow stronger.

Goal setting should be addressed within the framework of the recovery process. Even though I have come a long way in my recovery, I still have bad periods. Everybody does, even those who were not sexually abused. But judging from my observations and the reactions of those who are close to me, my bad days are more extreme than is usually expected.

There are days when it takes all my energy just to get out of bed or to perform a simple task. I never go out in public at night. I hate being in situations where I am among male strangers. I am uncomfortable in any situation where I am the only woman among a group of men, even if I know all of them. At times I still have nightmares and experience flashbacks. There are two places where I feel safe—at home and at work. Normally I choose not to enter other settings unless I am accompanied by someone who has gained my trust. I have learned to accept that this is okay. When I feel strong enough, I will institute changes. But in the meantime, I accept these limitations. I have learned to be patient during the healing process.

And I have learned to expect and accept setbacks. No one experiences a lifetime of perfection. Everyone has setbacks, whether or not they have been sexually abused. But survivors should expect setbacks because of the very nature of the experiences they are trying to overcome. Once the memories begin returning, and survivors are strong enough to work on their recovery, there will be moments of victory and moments of defeat. They shouldn't allow setbacks to permanently stop the progression.

As survivors become stronger, more memories will return. Judging from my experiences, the most devastating memories (apart from the initial recall of the abuse) return after the survivor has accepted the truth of the past. Recovering these memories can cause setbacks in healing. But as time passes, survivors adjust to the new memories, finally accept them, and grow stronger as they move toward recovery.

As I learned to accept my past, at some point I needed to know the whole truth. It wasn't until I accepted my most frightening memories—10 years into my recovery—that I was able to put together the bulk of the entire puzzle and begin to truly understand myself and the path my life had taken. At last I understood.

In reading other survivors' stories, I am amazed at how consistently their words capture my own thoughts and experiences. Survivors speak of how their abusers took away the life that would have been theirs and how they are unable to recapture that stolen part of their life. They speak of never becoming the person they might have been. Their words go far beyond the physical pain inflicted, reflecting the psychological, emotional, and spiritual fragmentation and loss of control that result from such attacks. In short, they speak of losing their dreams.

Suggestions for Survivors

- Try to accept that the abuse experiences were traumatic.
- Try to accept that the abuse experiences have affected many of the decisions you have made (even if you were repressing the memories).
- Try not to let others' expectations unduly influence you—doing so could put you at risk.
- Work on developing your ability to adapt to change.
- Try to accept that you suffered physical, psychological, emotional, and spiritual damage as a result of the abuse experiences.
- Try to accept that your actions (whether dictated consciously or unconsciously) ensured your continued survival.
- Try to understand that other survivors have experienced and feel similar things; you are not alone.
- Try to accept your limitations.
- Try to set reasonable goals.
- Learn to expect and accept setbacks in your recovery.
- Try to accept yourself as you are.
- Learn to think of yourself as a survivor, rather than a victim.

Suggestions for Friends and Family of Survivors

- Try to accept that tremendous damage was inflicted on survivors during the abuse experiences.

- Try to accept the idea that you don't understand what survivors must go through.
- Try not to place unfair demands upon survivors.
- Try to support survivors' decisions, whether or not you agree.

Conclusion

Misconception #9 is one of the worst fallacies surrounding the issue of childhood sexual abuse. In fact, sexual abuse affects every part of the child's life. Recently, I have come to understand how my abuse history colors my adult life. It impacted on every major decision I made, on every relationship I entered into, and on my ability to participate in activities—both before and after I recovered my memories.

Twelve years into recovery, I have finally begun to feel I know myself—who the child within me was before I was molested, and who I became as a result of the damage done by that traumatic event.

As I progressed with my recovery, my educational background helped me understand myself—the self that was lost as well as the self I have been, am now, and will become. My current task is to take back control of my life and become the person I want to be. As I integrate all the elements that make up my self—including the trauma experiences—I see that it's possible to reach that goal because I am moving toward becoming a whole person.

Through writing about my experiences, I am reaching out to other survivors in the hope that they can gain strength and insight from reading about my journey. That knowledge may help pave the way so their recovery process can begin. Further, I am attempting to educate those who have not been sexually abused. My hope is that they will come to accept the truth of the destructive nature of childhood sexual abuse and can then, in turn, offer the support survivors so desperately need.

Although I did not become a nurse, through my writing I have captured a part of the dream I lost. Serving as an instrument in the healing of other survivors has become my new dream.

"There is no failure except in no longer trying."
– Elbert Hubbard
American writer; 1856-1915

"If you bring forth what is within you, what you bring forth will save you. If you do not bring forth what is within you, what you do not bring forth will destroy you."
– Jesus,
in Elaine Pagels' *The Gnostic Gospel of Thomas*

9

Breaking Silence

*After reading an article I wrote about my abuse experiences,
a therapist said to me: "You have found your voice."
Only then did I realize how very difficult it is to talk about
being a survivor of childhood sexual abuse. In order to
adequately describe the experiences, we would have to create a
whole new language. But even then, only those who
spoke the same language could truly understand.*

Misconception #10: Their previous silence proves that both
child and adult survivors are lying.

Sexual abuse is not something most people—children or adults—
would lie about. Lying would gain them nothing. They would not be
able to describe in a convincing manner their fears, their feelings, or
what happened to them if it weren't the truth. Yet survivors often deny
any knowledge of the truth because of their youth or the dissociation,
repression, and other protective techniques they mastered during their
fight for survival. Once they stop denying, survivors understand when
they hear other survivors' stories; they constantly say, "She has to be
telling the truth because she described me."

Misconception #11: Abuse survivors should keep silent.

This idea is extremely harmful to survivors. Literature on recovery from childhood sexual abuse expounds the telling of a survivor's
personal story as an essential part of recovery. Survivors' testimony
points to the healing nature of disclosure. The only people who are

protected by survivors' continued silence are perpetrators and those who were not abused.

Both positive and negative disclosure experiences prove that the ideas presented in Misconceptions #10 and #11 are false.

* * * * *

Twelve years ago, at the end of a frustrating lovemaking session, I suddenly moaned and whispered, "I was sexually molested when I was a child." I was stunned. It was as if someone else had spoken, yet I knew the words were true. The room was filled with silence. At last my husband said, "Now I understand." He then talked about how he had known something was different about me from the first time we met, and now he had the key to understanding my sometimes bizarre behavior over the course of our 12-year marriage. His sensitivity and willingness to talk helped me feel safe as the shock of the initial memory seeped through me. Through the pain of discovery, at last I had broken my silence.

But as I began, at age 34, the journey toward self-discovery and recovery, I again cloaked myself in silence as the horror of my past washed through me. Like so many others who had gone before me, I was not yet strong enough to face the truth.

There are millions of sexually abused children who have not been recognized as such because their actions are calculated to protect them from discovery. It is common for these children to bury the terrible secret deep inside their subconscious minds because their psyches are too fragile to deal with the horror. In such cases, they wrap themselves in silence as a means of protecting themselves and their very fragmented world. The truth may be revealed to them in adulthood, when they are more able to handle it, when they finally understand all the things that baffled them about their behavior, when they learn to cope with and then begin their second fight for survival.

Whether the healing process begins in childhood or adulthood, it is a terrifying and lonely one. And it carries great risk because these survivors must now change the very behaviors that protected them from detection. Those who have been molested as children must learn to understand and accept before they can begin to heal. In order to succeed in life, they must learn to build themselves up instead of allowing themselves to be torn down. They must learn to value themselves when they feel they are of no value. They must learn to trust when the past tells them to do so brings pain and terror; to fail means they must live isolated and afraid.

Children who have been molested become the guardians of silence and the architects of deception. Such behavior helps to secure their safety and ensure their survival. That silence, that secrecy, protects the abused child and his or her family, yet I am convinced continued silence prevents the adult survivor from healing. I know this was true in my own case.

Several years after my memories returned and, in shock, I whispered the truth to my husband, I reached a point where I needed to unburden myself, to come out of the darkness and be bathed in the light. I knew I had to again break my silence and reveal the secret. And yet there was risk. How would people react? Would I be believed? Could I trust them to safeguard my dreadful secret? And how could I open up and talk about something that I, as a child, was threatened to keep silent about?

Finally, about 6 years ago, I decided to tell my secret to my closest friend. I viewed this as a healthy sign, that I had at least partially begun to place responsibility for the attack on the perpetrator and I was trying to release the shame.

We had known each other 16 years, and had collaborated on several non-fiction writing projects. As we began working on fiction together, we dug deep within ourselves and reached a level of incredible mental connection where it seemed we could read each others' minds even when we were far apart. Often I would call her to discuss a problem I was having with a plot line of a novel. She would respond, "I have been thinking about that and here's what I've come up with ..." even though she was editing a different part of the novel. It was almost spooky how frequently our thoughts were focused on the same topic, but we accepted and eventually came to rely on that strong mental connection.

After receiving sympathy and understanding from my husband years earlier when he learned my secret, I expected no less from my friend. Finally I told her what happened to me. I needed her support, but she responded by telling me about her house being robbed many years earlier. Her reaction stunned and hurt me. She didn't encourage me to talk about my pain, but instead told me about her feelings of invasion and her fear for her son—who wasn't even home at the time of the break-in. As I listened, she voiced her fears for a child now grown, and I realized she couldn't comprehend what had happened to me.

I let her finish her story, and then said, "Years later you are still afraid for that little boy who wasn't a part of the robbery. You lost only possessions and the sanctity of your home. I lost the sanctity of my body!"

We then talked about my pain, but it was not the beginning I had envisioned. I learned to be prepared for the unexpected when making disclosures, and that even those closest to me might not understand. Again I wrapped myself in silence.

The response of my friend was not unusual, I have learned. Therapist Kathy Duguid of Menlo Park, California, [1] who works extensively with incest survivors, cautions, "Some people can't take this stuff. Tell intimate friends and people whom you want to tell only if it appears they can deal with it." She also warns, "Be careful who you disclose to. Know your motives—don't set yourself up to be abused again." Another therapist working with incest survivors, Bobbi Hoover of Santa Clara, California, [2] points out that disclosure to friends is often "less problematic than to family. Friends are with you because they want to be; they aren't 'stuck' with you" like family members are.

In disclosing to my friend, I had not prepared her for what was to come. I had simply blurted everything out, not recognizing her need to brace herself. I also hadn't understood that she might not be able to deal with what I wanted to confide in her. Nor had I told her what I needed from her. Unintentionally, in ignorance, I set the stage for failure.

After that unsuccessful disclosure, it was quite a while before I could tell anyone else. I eventually broke my silence again when a family member to whom I had been very close in my growing-up years pressured me into disclosing, then accused me of lying. It was the worst possible scenario and caused me a great deal of pain.

I couldn't imagine anyone accusing a survivor of lying about being sexually abused as a child. I couldn't imagine what someone who was not abused would have to gain from lying about being sexually abused. It is hard enough for survivors to come to terms with the degradation, humiliation, grief, pain, horror, blame, shame. Why would someone bring this upon herself?

I lived through this new turmoil and eventually got beyond it. Later I came to understand that both this family member and the close friend I had earlier disclosed to were denying the severity of what happened because they couldn't accept the hurt I suffered. They didn't want it to have happened to me. Further, I began to realize those who have no experience with childhood sexual abuse probably wonder why those who are abused have been silent.

Children remain silent because they are afraid—that no one will believe them, that they will be blamed, that they will be removed from their home, that someone in their family will be harmed, that dad will be put in jail for not taking care of them, that mom will no longer love them. Children are bowed by the horrible power, both physically and psychologically, exerted by the perpetrator, and by the awful things they now feel about themselves. They are silent because they are ashamed and feel tremendous guilt. I was also silent because I feared my attacker would fulfill his promise—that he would kill me or my mother, or that he would fulfill the unspoken threat and kill my younger sister.

Adult survivors are silent for many of the same reasons that plague children. But in addition, as in my case, many adult survivors repress the memories for years. Some survivors don't begin retrieving their memories until very late in life (sixties or seventies or beyond).

If I had known better, I would have started disclosing with people I was sure could handle hearing my painful story. Kathy Duguid advises, "Get support from therapists, Incest Survivors Anonymous, and survivors' groups. People with experience provide the best support. Those without experience can't give the type of support you need." She also notes that people who have been abused in other ways (physically or emotionally) can be supportive if they have gone through recovery. However, if they haven't worked through their own issues, they may feel revictimized when they listen to the disclosure.

When making a disclosure, survivors should choose their audience carefully, making sure the person being disclosed to respects and cares for them, has their well-being in mind, is someone they shared things with in the past, is a person they trust, and is someone they feel safe with. It may also be wise for survivors to find a way of warning this person that they are feeling vulnerable and being specific about just what it is they need from this person.

When considering disclosing, survivors need to be aware of their physical and psychological boundaries. They need to select a place where they feel comfortable and a time during which the conversation won't be interrupted.

When survivors reach an appropriate stage (well into their recovery), disclosing will allow them to release the poisons that have been bottled up inside them for so long. It is also important to disclose because the acceptance and positive feedback of others helps survivors learn to accept and value themselves. However, survivors need to be sure they undertake disclosure when they are strong and doing it for themselves.

Bobbi Hoover concurs, "Choose an appropriate place to disclose—boundaries are a major issue. And always do it one hundred percent for the survivor. Expect little back. If you get back a lot, that's wonderful."

If survivors are disclosing incest, Kathy Duguid offers a caution when telling family members. "In the family situation, one child might have been abused while the siblings weren't. If the siblings had a different (positive) experience with the abuser, they may not believe you." Also, family members sometimes offer support—as long as the survivor remains silent.

With all the grief attached to disclosure, it seems logical to ask: Why would survivors in their right minds voluntarily put themselves through this process? Because disclosure is one of the keys to healing. It allows the survivor to free himself from this terrible horror, to release the pain, to share the burden. And when disclosure is met with caring and support, it eventually allows the survivor to release the guilt and shame. That is an incredibly empowering experience!

As with much of recovery, however, there is pain along with the joy. I learned this lesson through my initial disclosures, and I, again, wrapped myself in silence. Several years passed before I took the next step in disclosure. And this step was motivated by guilt and fear. Had my much-younger sister been molested, too? When I escaped my attacker by moving out of my parents' house at age 22, my sister was 13—the same age I initially believed I was when my terror began. I became tormented by fear that she might even now be experiencing the same pain I suffered.

Finally, I told her my secret and learned, thankfully, that history had not repeated itself. But when I refused to divulge the man's name, she provided it. She had sensed his malevolence without knowing what I had suffered at his hands. Once her shock wore off, her understanding and caring served as sources of great comfort to me. During that conversation, we reversed roles as she became the "big sister." At last I felt accepted, no longer alone with my pain. There was truly relief in the telling.

With this relief and the good feelings that came from being believed, I gained confidence and self-esteem. Eventually I decided to tell three of my women friends, separately, what had been done to me. When I did, they each confided their own stories of childhood sexual abuse. These women are all college-educated professionals whose outward lives mask the horror that has been a part of their inner selves. As in my case, no one would suspect it happened to them.

Although disclosing the story of my long-term sexual abuse has helped me tremendously, I firmly believe that survivors must freely choose to tell. Disclosure is not something that should be mandated by well-meaning friends, family, the press, or circumstances out of the survivor's control. Bobbi Hoover concurs: "Do it for you." She says, "Choose your time frame. You've got to be ready on so many levels. Doing it too soon will set you back."

Although each survivor goes through healing at her or his own rate, and chooses the stages of recovery, disclosure can be a very large part of the healing process. My early attempts at disclosure brought degrees of victory as well as defeat, and I learned to look upon the healing process as one of discovery and growth. Often it involves taking two steps forward and one step back. But as long as any gain is made, I feel I'm succeeding.

* * * * *

Two years ago, I reached the stage where further healing had to come from sharing my experiences in a more public domain. As with confiding in friends and family, there is a tremendous risk with public disclosure—even as adults, we may not be believed. But beyond the belief factor, there is further risk. Once survivors have publicly disclosed, they can't take it back; and, depending on where they disclose, their world may radically change. They may be humiliated, ridiculed, or rejected.

As I considered publicly disclosing, certain words kept coming to mind: finding a safe place, trust, control. Even when survivors feel safe with the incident of public disclosure, trust themselves and the people they are disclosing to, and maintain control, they may not get the result they hoped for. There is pain involved with disclosure, but there is also triumph! I have found the more I talk about the past, the easier it becomes. It's as if a small piece of the burden breaks away, freeing me, each time I confide in someone.

In my case, initially the issue of public disclosure centered around whether or not to disclose at work. The work setting had always been a safe place for me, one where I was respected and where I maintained control. The issue regarding disclosure at work first surfaced when I began publishing articles in *The Healing Woman* newsletter under a pen name.

I am a staff member at a university where faculty are required to publish, and their professional achievements are well publicized. Whenever my articles or books were published, I sought equal recognition. But suddenly, my strong professional belief that staff deserve recognition for their private accomplishments, in part to allow them to be viewed and valued as "whole" people, was at odds with my personal need for privacy.

After careful consideration, I decided to let it be known in my work setting that I had published articles dealing with recovery from childhood sexual abuse. Although it removed the veil that protected me in that setting, I received powerful, supportive feedback.

Also, as the leader of several staff self-help groups, I utilized those forums to further my own recovery and to help others. When my writing was presented as part of a women's studies course by a counselor/professor colleague, four college students were moved to verbally disclose, for the first time, their personal histories of childhood incest. These students were fortunate because their professor holds a Ph.D. in psychology. She was able to deal with the unexpected disclosures, then she privately assisted the students through the emotional outpouring. Most professors are not trained to handle such situations.

My disclosure at work was an empowering experience, and so far it has been positive. Part of the success stems from the fact that the people being disclosed to have a degree of protection—they are not members of my family or my close personal friends, thus they do not have as great a stake in my well-being. And because of that distance, they are able to really listen and then give comfort and support. They care, but there is no great personal risk for them.

Despite the uplifting side to public disclosure, I am well aware the time may come when I experience a negative encounter that will bring on a return of nightmares and sap my confidence and self-esteem. And such a setback might rob me of the ability to progress for a period of time. I move cautiously, carefully selecting how, when, and where to disclose. And I have consciously chosen not to disclose to some people.

When my boss asked specific questions about *The Healing Woman* newsletter before I decided to disclose at my place of work, I declined to answer, and he accepted my decision. Later, when I realized the rage I felt for my attacker was so near the surface that it might affect my job performance, I confided in him. He was very understanding and supportive.

To date, I have chosen not to confide in many men. I may need to work on this issue in the future, but I know I am not ready at the present time. I felt it was a major victory when I learned to accept, despite how far I have come, that there are still limitations on my ability to disclose.

I view the possible negative side of public disclosure as a risk I must take in order to progress, and I am always prepared for negative responses. I am also aware that public disclosure is not something that should be attempted at the early stages of healing. It took me 10 years to feel ready to begin this phase of the journey toward recovery. Some survivors never reach this point in healing.

As I have seen through my own experiences, talking about the abuse is a means of regaining control. As disclosing has become easier, I am more willing to share. The positive feedback received through public disclosure has helped me hold my head up high and understand I was not to blame.

But disclosure is difficult, even under the best circumstances. It is often accompanied by physical reactions such as those I experienced—blood rushing to the face, a rapid increase in heartbeat, feeling lightheaded, a quivering voice that sounds far away and projects an unfamiliar pitch, and, finally, uncontrolled crying. But the more I disclose, the milder these reactions become.

I measure the success of disclosure in my own healing process by the ways I have changed. I am now usually in complete control whenever I disclose, and I no longer cry when I talk with others about my past. Often, lately, the disclosure is made without any advance planning on my part. It now seems like a natural occurrence because I no longer feel ashamed. Often the discussions begin with my story but end up encompassing the whole issue of sexual abuse: the frequency of occurrence; changing public views; current court cases; movies or television shows that deal with the issue; changing laws; why abusers do such things. It's not just about me anymore, and I think that's a giant step forward.

* * * * *

For years, I refused to tell my parents about the abuse because I didn't want them to suffer from guilt over not protecting or understanding their daughter. But two family members knew, and at last I caved in to the pressure to disclose. Their reaction—anger, but not shock or surprise—led me to believe they had already been told. They believed me, but it was difficult for us to talk. And my father's angry *"Who did it?"* kept pounding through me. I didn't want to divulge the name. I was still afraid I would not be believed. The conversation with my parents triggered the recurrence of the nightmares I had experienced for many months after the memories first returned, nightmares that I hadn't experienced in years. I began to fear the healing had ended.

One year later, I was again able to talk to my parents about the sexual abuse. I began trying to help them deal with their questions and anguish, and I am still trying to help them understand what I felt and experienced. I am trying to help ease my mother's pain over not knowing. And I am trying to help my father accept that I could not seek his intervention.

I have not yet found the words to convey to him my paralyzing fear at the time the abuse happened, and later my sense of fragmentation and guilt, my need to protect our family, my fear of not being believed. I haven't explained that I couldn't talk because of the death threats— that even now I can feel my attacker's fingers applying pressure on my throat, that at times I still fear I will suffocate from the constriction in my throat. I don't think anything I say will ever remove my father's pain. He believes that he is responsible, that he did not protect his child. And yet it was not his fault any more than it was mine.

Recently I found out that my parents have learned the name of the man who hurt me. I don't blame my sister for finally telling them; she had lived with their pain as they scrutinized each of their friends, wondering "Is he the one?" Their new understanding allows them to share things about this man that I hadn't known; and as they begin drawing their own conclusions, I get the sense that now they believe at a deeper level.

As my sense of security grows, I have started to tell them some of what this man did to me over the years. When I related one incident that occurred when I was 22, they both remembered witnessing the ending of the scene and feeling their own disquiet at the time, although neither had suspected the truth. It gave us a shared moment of understanding and made me realize I had taken another step toward healing: I am no longer protecting my family from the truth of the past. I know they will survive, just as I have.

Suggestions for Survivors

- Make sure you are well along in your recovery before you decide to disclose.
- Carefully choose who you are going to disclose to.
- Carefully plan the disclosure.
- Try not to allow yourself to be pressured into disclosing before you are ready.
- Try not to allow yourself to be pressured into disclosing to people with whom you would prefer not to share your secrets.
- Maintain control of the disclosure experience.

- Prepare the person before you disclose.
- Be prepared for a negative reaction so you won't be devastated if it happens.
- Try not to expect too much of those who are closest to you; they may be overwhelmed by your disclosure.
- Surround yourself with a group of caring people with whom you can share your experiences (people who have a degree of distance).
- Try to understand that disclosure is essential for recovery and healing; it is an empowering experience, one through which you can release the hidden poisons from your body.
- Be careful about making decisions regarding public disclosure; once you have spoken, you can't take it back and your world may change radically.

Suggestions for Friends and Family of Survivors

When a survivor discloses his or her history of childhood sexual abuse, friends and family may experience a wide range of feelings, including shock and outrage. But you must try to control your reactions and remain sensitive to the needs of the survivor. Unless the survivor is well on the way to recovery and healing, the response of friends and family will have a major impact on her or his peace of mind and immediate ability to continue to heal. Remember, abuse takes place in isolation, while recovery takes place after the survivor seeks the support of others.

Because so much depends on the reactions of those whom survivors confide in, I have provided additional details about many of the following suggestions.

- Listen, no matter how uncomfortable you feel.
- Believe the survivor.
- Accept that whatever happened is destructive. Much of the lasting damage comes from terror, especially that which is associated with the threat of being killed.
- Try to understand the survivor was not to blame, could not have prevented the abuse, and should not be made to feel ashamed. Although survivors should know on a rational level that they were not to blame, they do blame themselves for a very long time. Through accepting and understanding, friends and family will help the survivor release the shame.
- Show concern by asking if the survivor is all right and how to help. Accept the situation if all the survivor wants others to do

is listen. Friends and family should try to understand they can't "fix it."

- Try not to sympathize with the abuser. Offering such an opinion will undercut support and reinforce the survivor's negative feelings.
- Let the survivor cry (or express anger, fear, sadness). This is what friends are for! Also, try to understand that the survivor is going to express a wide range of conflicting emotions. This may result in opposing behaviors such as survivors feeling compassionate and protective of others yet being enraged at those closest to them. Disclosure will impact on relationships friends and family have with survivors.
- Touch an arm or hold the survivor's hand. Hug the survivor if she indicates such a gesture is welcome. But ask first, especially if there is any doubt about whether the survivor wants to be touched (particularly if friends and family are the same sex as the attacker). The survivor will indicate what she needs, and it is important to honor her boundaries. Offering physical comfort will help the survivor understand that she is not physically repulsive and that she is worthy of being loved.
- Try to understand what the survivor is saying when he doesn't divulge everything. This may entail some reading between the lines. Those close to the survivor may want to know specifics that he isn't willing to discuss, including the perpetrator's name. Let the survivor dictate the parameters for disclosure.
- Friends and family should release their own emotions. They could let the survivor know they hurt for her, are outraged, or whatever else they feel that offers support and is genuine. But they shouldn't lose control or they will add to the survivor's burden. They should try to make sure their emotions (anger, desire for revenge, etc.) are expressed in ways that aren't frightening or threatening to the survivor. It is also important that friends and family seek professional help for themselves if they are not able to deal with the situation. Adding their problems to the survivor's could set the stage for the destruction of the relationship.
- Friends and family shouldn't blame themselves for not knowing what happened, especially if they were close to the survivor at the time the abuse took place. Seldom do others suspect.
- Friends and family should learn as much as they can about childhood sexual abuse and its aftermath. Not only will this action show support for survivors, but it will enable them to

better understand survivors' behavior and learn to recognize the changes survivors must go through as they strive for recovery and healing.

- Encourage the survivor to seek professional help, but accept the limitations he sets. Each survivor must find his own path to recovery.
- Friends and family should not betray the survivor's confidence. Survivors must be allowed to choose the people they confide in and to control the circumstances surrounding disclosure.
- Allow the survivor to set the guidelines for participation in the recovery process. Not doing so could put the survivor at risk and impede healing.

Conclusion

Misconceptions #10 and #11 have a particularly dangerous affect on the well-being of survivors. Accusing them of lying could destroy their peace of mind and self-confidence and seriously hamper their recovery efforts. Expecting them to remain silent after they have reached the stage where they need to talk about their past is unfair and harmful. Such expectations demand that they continue to keep the poison inside them. The only possible explanation for wanting a survivor to remain silent is that such an action protects those who were not abused from knowing the truth. It also protects perpetrators from being discovered.

These two misconceptions must be wholeheartedly discounted both by survivors who want to heal and by a society that wants to comprehend and end these horrible crimes.

As I have progressed with my healing and the issue has become less about me and more about childhood sexual abuse in general, I am now aware of the responsibility of survivors to help each other. Through sharing, survivors can provide caring, understanding, and confirmation; they can assist in guiding others through the healing process by providing examples of men and women who are recovering. Through sharing, survivors can also help remove the burdens of guilt, responsibility, and shame.

And survivors must assume an equally weighty responsibility regarding today's and tomorrow's children. By speaking out, by making the problem known, they can help to change public opinion and bring about a revision in the laws that govern the crimes of childhood sexual abuse. Survivors can advocate to see that perpetrators are prosecuted with vigor and that the legal system, at the same time, protects the children. As more survivors come together and raise their joint voices, they will become a tremendous force in implementing change.

The ultimate goal is to snap the chain of childhood sexual abuse. To be forewarned is to be forearmed. Through breaking silence, and revealing the dark secret, survivors can help to create a world in which future generations of children will not suffer from these heinous crimes. Through their raised voices, survivors can help create a world in which children do not have to search for a safe place to make their own.

"Once somebody listens, you don't have to shout anymore."
– Alice Miller,
from an interview with *The Healing Woman*

"Why do we keep hiding our deepest feelings from each other? We suffer much, but we also have great gifts of healing for each other. The mystery is that by hiding our pain, we also hide our ability to heal."
– Henri J. Nouwen
The Road to Daybreak

10

Through the Eyes of the Beholder

In disregarding the truth, one is tied to darkness.
Through wrapping oneself in the truth—no matter how
horrible—one is eventually bathed in light.

Misconception #12: If survivors lead fulfilling lives, then
everything is okay.

In observing survivors' outer selves, one sees only the picture
they present to the world. In some cases, they are still repressing. In
other cases, they must cling to that more perfect picture of themselves
because they are in denial. In still other cases, that outer self reflects
what they wish the inner self could be. For survivors, very rarely is the
outward picture the true one. Abused children perfect the act of
deception in order to keep the deed from being detected. After years
of leading a lie, even after the memories return, it is very easy for adult
survivors to present a picture of a whole person. The truth is, they are
breaking apart inside.

* * * * *

I hate having my picture taken! And I'm usually not photogenic.
Lately I have come to suspect the two are related. Although I used to
look much younger than my actual age (I was asked to present my
driver's license as proof of my age until I turned 30), I usually look
much older in photographs.

When I am forced to have my picture taken, I am terribly
uncomfortable, especially when it occurs in public settings. I have
finally come to understand that my aversion to having my picture

taken is related to my history of childhood sexual abuse. Over a period of 12 years, during a time when I should have been excited and curious about the physical changes I was experiencing, my emotional growth was stunted by my attacker's continual terrorization. Instead of taking pleasure in growing up, I felt terrible things about my body and myself. My identity was destroyed by my attacker. The abuse experiences became the core of the new identify I worked so hard to develop. They were the center of my being, and they seeped through every part of me.

I repressed the truth of the attacks because I was unable to deal with it, but I was haunted by dark images that I didn't understand. Those dark images colored the way I viewed myself. I have always thought of myself as having an ugly body and an ugly face. I have always felt dirty and scarred. I believed others made fun of me behind my back. I felt they could see the things about me that I could only feel. I believed they could sense my guilt and shame even when I could not name the cause.

I felt my inner conflict colored my outer self, and I was unconsciously afraid it would be captured by the camera. In my view, my torment is captured in photos because I usually take horrible pictures.

In a discussion with one of my aunts, some time after I had disclosed to her my history of childhood sexual abuse, she expressed impatience with the slowness of my progress toward recovery. She couldn't understand why it was taking so long for me to come to terms with my past. I think she believed I was using the abuse experience as an excuse for whatever was wrong with my life.

I now realize that I shouldn't have expected her to understand how my history of abuse affected every important aspect of my life and molded me into the person I became. Only those who have been abused can understand my anger—that I felt my body, my self, my life, my future were stolen from me. Only those who have been abused can understand my torment, my fear, or why I chose to lead an isolated life. Only those who have been abused can understand that, no matter how hard I tried or how quickly I healed, I could never retrieve what was taken from me. Only those who have been abused can understand that, no matter how successful I became at building a new life, I could never be the person I might have been.

As I talked with my aunt, it became obvious that she had no idea what I was going through. And I couldn't find the right words to help her understand. Frustrated, I blurted out: "I am ugly!"

She was stunned by my words, then recovered and said, "You are not ugly, and I have the pictures to prove it!" I listened as she related her view of my physical appearance, and then I spoke about mine. Since our opinions were diametrically opposed, it quickly became apparent that we saw two different women. She saw the contented, successful projection while I saw the tormented, angry one. She saw the niece she loved, while I saw a contaminated, scarred, ugly "thing."

A short time after the discussion with my aunt, I received an envelope filled with pictures of my growing-up years. An enclosed letter put forth her case, and declared that I couldn't possibly believe the child in those pictures was ugly or that the young woman who was seen growing into adulthood was deeply troubled. She contended the only picture in which I was ugly was the most recent one, the one that had appeared in a local newspaper in conjunction with an article discussing the publication of my first book. She didn't know that picture was taken shortly after my memories began returning.

I looked at the pictures and saw what she saw in the early ones— a happy, safe, secure child. I realized those pictures were taken before I was molested. The pictures taken after I was molested appeared "tainted." When I looked at them, I saw a child, teenager, or young adult who was uncomfortable with herself. To me, the camera captured my feelings of dishonor, contamination, torment, and infection. In many of the photos, even when I am smiling, my eyes reflected the pain trapped within me.

I then thought of the pictures that were missing, the ones that recorded some of the important moments in my life, ones I associate with an "ugly" me. All those pictures (taken between the ages of 17 and 22) reflect a woman who looks 30 years old and is extremely uncomfortable with herself. The settings for these pictures were my high school prom, my high school graduation, my college homecoming, a college fashion panel, two friends' weddings where I served as bridesmaids, and my own wedding.

I can think of only one photo taken during this period of time that I consider to be a reflection of what I hope I really looked like—my passport photo, taken at age 19. I suspect it turned out quite well because I was embarking on an exciting adventure, one I had long dreamed of undertaking. The difference could also be attributed to my unconscious awareness that, at least temporarily, I was escaping my attacker.

Very few pictures exist of me between the ages of 23 and 46, and most of them are okay because I have learned to control the setting.

* * * * *

In thinking back on the conversation with my aunt, I learned a great deal about how those who were not sexually abused view survivors. She saw the outer me, the whole person I have always tried to present to the world. Even when she knew the truth about how the private person was shattered, she still saw what she wanted to see. Even after I told her how I felt and what I had experienced, she had no point of reference that would allow her to understand how sexual abuse colors survivors' lives. It was easier for her to cling to the belief that I was all right, that the attacks and terrorization had no long-lasting effect, than to try to accept what I was saying. It was simply too painful for her to know what I had been through.

Unfortunately, at that time I couldn't adequately put into words the depth of my feelings of destruction. I was frustrated by my inability to help her understand. As time has passed, I have been able to verbalize my feelings more clearly. I hope my aunt has learned that survivors of childhood sexual abuse look at their outer selves through eyes that see the truth of what happened to them, even when they are still repressing the memories. They see themselves through a prism that reflects their hurt, pain, anguish, guilt, blame, fear, torment, shame. They are unable to separate in their mind's eye the inner person (who has been damaged) from the outer person (who may appear whole). I feel the camera captured my invisible self, including my inner torment. To me, it presented an ugly picture because it captured my soul.

My aunt's inability to understand might have placed undue pressure on me to "see it her way." Early in my disclosure process, my recovery was negatively impacted by the unrealistic expectations of people close to me who couldn't possibly understand what it takes to recover from childhood sexual abuse. I learned the hard way not to bow to pressure applied by others because accepting their deadlines for recovery can result in tremendous setbacks. When I felt pressured to heal quickly, I measured myself by my failure to meet others' goals. I began to doubt that I would ever heal.

Accepting the pressure of others' expectations prevented me from feeling good about myself, from embracing my small victories, from understanding the tragedy of what I had experienced as a child, from appreciating the enormity of the task I had undertaken in choosing to recover. Their pressure made me doubt my suffering, and it called into question my entire healing process, the process that had ensured my continued survival. Finally I realized their expectations were for them, not for me. They needed me to be healthy and normal. Since this healing was about me, their expectations shouldn't have mattered. In discounting their wishes, I was able to continue to heal.

In accepting the inability of those closest to me to understand, I released myself from the need to meet their expectations. And I learned to expect less from them, thus eliminating the possibility of any negative scenario over their failure to live up to my expectations. This freed all of us. It allowed them to wish for my healing without it hampering my recovery, and it allowed me to care for them without seeing them through the prism of my need for their support. In removing their responsibility for participation in my ongoing healing process, I have moved forward; and they have been able to share in and celebrate my progress.

* * * * *

At the time the conversation with my aunt took place, I thought I hadn't been able to communicate to her the pain I felt or the way I viewed myself. In that instance, I believed the true picture was the one I held, and I felt it was essential that she be able to view me through my eyes. But I failed to change her picture of me. Now I realize she shouldn't be expected to instantly understand what has taken me years to comprehend. I have been working on the puzzle that was my life and my self since the memories began returning at age 34. When measured against that standard, her access to information regarding my past occurred relatively recently.

As the years passed and I grew stronger, I was able to address my aunt's concerns regarding my recovery. Now I realize she constantly challenged my recovery. Seeking answers to the questions she previously raised forced me to grow, facing the demons that resided within me. This realization called to mind a stress workshop I attended. The counselor doing the presentation drew a picture on the blackboard of what statisticians would call a bell-shaped curve. The line delineating the left side of the curve was marked with tiny slashes that represent positive life stressors that challenge us. The top of the bell denoted the maximum level of stress under which we can maintain stability. The right side of the curve was marked with slashes that represent life stressors that put us beyond the state of coping.

The bottom left side of the curve represented the state of minimum stress—where we are unchallenged, bored. The bottom right side of the curve represented the state of maximum stress—where we are totally out of control. Each individual attending the workshop was asked to name the stressors in her life that are represented by the positive and negative slash marks. The most desirable picture to strive for is a curve (representing one's life) where stressors line the left side of the bell almost to the top. Such a scenario represents a challenging and rewarding set of life circumstances, but one that is not overly stressful.

Another of life's challenges is the dichotomy between pain and triumph. This dichotomy is illustrated on a Post-It® notepad that sits on my desk at work. The picture, drawn by an artist named Boynton, depicts a small animal positioned at the middle of a tall staircase. He is struggling to climb the next step, which is as high as he is long. It shows his head and front paws on the top of the step while his body dangles down the front of the step. The inscription reads: "No pain, no gain."

I don't mean to suggest that survivors should intentionally inflict pain upon themselves in a self-punishing manner. Recovering memories and/or facing a past that includes childhood sexual abuse is a painful process, as is undertaking recovery and healing. Each step should be taken slowly, cautiously, with full knowledge that it will result in pain.

But survivors should also bear in mind that only through addressing the truth, and accepting the accompanying pain, can they grow stronger and become whole; only through confronting the past can they regain their sense of self. Without pain, survivors experience very little in the way of triumph.

As I applied the theories of the stress curve and the pain/triumph dichotomy to my relationship with my aunt, I realized in the early years of recovery, when I was weak, I learned to ignore her expectations. In later years, through dealing with her expectations (and overcoming them), I made remarkable strides toward healing. Her probing became an integral part of my healing journey. Without it, I would have felt less pain; but there also would have been less triumph, and my recovery would have been even slower.

I have often reflected on the conversation concerning the photos, and I realize we both gained something from that exchange. It was important to me that my aunt begin to understand the magnitude of the difficulties I have faced in attempting to recover. Because the terrorization was enacted over a period of 12 years, the damage to my psyche was extensive. In fact, my sense of self was totally destroyed.

It was important to me that my aunt understand my life-long task has been to create a new identity for myself, one that includes the terror, the damage to my body, the trashing of my soul. I wanted her to understand that I cannot become the niece she wants me to be. And I now want her to understand that one of the tasks I must face is to move beyond the contaminated identity and embrace the woman I am, a woman who was abused as a child but who has incorporated the memories and is moving beyond those experiences.

It is also important to me that my aunt recognize how significant each of my gains is—no matter how small. I feel she now understands my successes, and perhaps she is capable of measuring them because she no longer applies pressure on me to recover. I think she now trusts that I am moving forward as rapidly as I can.

And I am now able to view my aunt's original assessment of me in a different light than I could at the time she issued the challenge. Now that the pain of recovering my memories is not so all-consuming, I understand that her assessment centered around my strong points, which I had negated. Also, she saw the goodness in me that I felt had been destroyed by the attacks. Lately, through listening to the counsel of those close to me, I am once again able to recognize my strengths and honor them.

I now realize it was not only important that my aunt understand me, but it is essential that I see myself through her eyes. I must try to strike a balance between her image of me and mine. As I grow stronger and gain self-esteem, I am more clearly able to see how she viewed me, and I realize beauty truly is in the eyes of the beholder.

Suggestions for Survivors

- Try to discount undue pressure applied by others.
- Try to disregard unreasonable expectations of others.
- Try to turn negative experiences into positive growth opportunities.
- Accept stressors that challenge but don't overburden the recovery process.
- Try to listen to the positive feedback of others.

Suggestions for Friends and Family of Survivors

- Try to accept that a survivor who appears "normal" and "under control" may be breaking apart inside.
- Look for signs that the survivor is hurting and ask how to help.
- Listen to survivors and learn how they view themselves.
- Try not to discount what survivors say.
- Try to accept that a survivor's view of himself is very real to the survivor.
- Try not to apply pressure on survivors to heal.

Conclusion

Survivors lead anything but the "normal" lives others see. Like many survivors, I was intent upon presenting to the world a picture that is the opposite of what I was feeling and experiencing. No one close to me had any idea that I had been sexually abused as a child. My actions were designed to prevent detection.

But once a survivor discloses the truth of what happened, those who share the "secret" can have a large impact on the survivor's recovery process. My experiences have shown that even negative encounters can eventually have a positive influence. Through interacting with my aunt, I came to realize her picture of me offered a degree of comfort in the journey toward recovery.

As I have begun to heal, I realize my mind's eye image reflected the hurt person I was; her mind's eye image reflects the person I am striving to become. In recent months, as I look in the mirror, I frequently see the woman she sees—one who is not ugly, one who is not scarred. I am beginning to wonder which image of me would now be captured by the lens of a camera.

"There are two ways of spreading light: to be the candle or the mirror that reflects it."

– Edith Wharton,
American novelist, 1862-1937

"You gain strength, courage, and confidence by every experience in which you really stop to look fear in the face. You are able to say to yourself, 'I lived through this horror. I can take the next thing that comes along.' You must do the thing you think you cannot do."

– Eleanor Roosevelt

11

Breaking the Cycle of Sexual Abuse

*Surviving childhood sexual abuse challenges all our
resources. Often, I felt I could not endure the existence
I was trapped in or summon the strength to go through another
day. And yet I lived, and eventually I broke the cycle
of abuse. Now that I have come this far, I recognize my own
brand of courage and I know I will survive!*

Misconception #13: Childhood sexual abuse is about sex.

Absolutely not! As is often said about rape, childhood sexual
abuse is about power, control, total disregard of boundaries and
personal integrity, and fear.

Misconception #14: If it only happened once, what's the
problem? Survivors live through it, don't they? Why do they
allow it to ruin the rest of their lives?

Living through it isn't enough! Survivors have to work on all the
issues surrounding the attack and the ramifications that resulted from
it. The information presented in this chapter will show that childhood
sexual abuse isn't about sex and, for many survivors, sexual abuse
doesn't just happen once or by a single perpetrator.

* * * * *

Ten years into my healing journey, I began writing a series of
articles for *The Healing Woman* newsletter that explored my ongoing
recovery from childhood sexual abuse. At that point, I thought there
was nothing left to remember. But I was wrong. I was forced to deal

with current demons as more and more details were uncovered. And I would once again be plunged into a nightmare existence as my brain reenacted scenes from long ago when I was physically, mentally, emotionally, and spiritually violated.

Mid-way through writing one of the articles, I remembered being sexually molested a second time, 24 years earlier, when I was 20 years old and taking a semester of college aboard a ship while traveling around the world. Early in the voyage, during a period of rough weather when most passengers were below deck in their cabins, I sought some fresh air in an attempt to calm my upset stomach. The perpetrator, a member of the ship's crew—a man I did not know—caught me alone, pinned me against the wall, and sexually molested me.

He grabbed at my breasts, squeezing and scratching them; he rubbed my crotch with his hand, then thrust his throbbing penis against it; he kissed me violently, then thrust his tongue into my mouth. Throughout the ordeal, I hit him and tried to push him away; but he was far stronger than I was, and my efforts proved futile. And my cries of anguish went unanswered.

When it was over, I was horrified to see the look in his eyes. He had thrived on my fear and revulsion! He loved his physical and mental power over me. He "got off" on knowing he had invaded my privacy and my person. I felt totally degraded, as if he was the master and I was his slave.

As he released me, his ugly laughter reverberated through me, and his taunting boast that he could "have" me whenever he wanted shot fear through my entire being.

Although the ugly encounter traumatized me, at the time I had no memory of being sexually molested when I was a child. Afterward, I was silent because I blamed myself for being alone, for putting myself in such a position; in short, I blamed myself for inviting such an attack. My self-esteem was further destroyed, and I suffered from guilt and a deep sense of shame. But my greatest fear was that I might not be able to avoid him in the confines of a ship that looked big when compared to tugboats but was dwarfed by cruise ships.

My fear was heightened that night, when an intruder unlocked my door and rummaged around the cabin. Although I slept through the incident, my roommate (who occupied the top bunk) was awakened and silently waited for him to leave. Then she awakened me and told me what had happened. I said nothing about the attack on me, and the next day she identified the intruder (my attacker) to our stewardess, who berated him and took steps to see that the women's cabin keys were kept away from the male crew members.

Although nothing seemed to be missing from the cabin, I suspect he took a personal item—a token of his conquest.

Hoping the stewardess' warning would protect me from further harm, but fearing the worst, I cautiously moved about the ship, taking a companion with me whenever possible. But I had to walk to class alone, and often he would appear in front of me at those times. He laughed at my fear, leered, and grabbed at me. And then he would let me pass. When I was with my friends, his too-wide grin made me cringe. On several occasions, when he was with fellow crew members, he pointed at me. I could tell by his lowered voice, the look in his eyes, the indication of his head, and their laughter that he told stories about me. It was worse than humiliating. The more he enjoyed the game of tormenting me, the more introverted I became. I felt like a trapped animal. And we had barely begun the voyage that was to last four months.

As we traveled south from Los Angeles toward Peru, a friend told me about a big celebration that would soon take place. As every ship crosses the equator, those passengers who have never done so before are forced to participate in a ritual centering around King Neptune. My friend, who had gone through the initiation years earlier, wouldn't tell me anything more, and I feared what the day would bring. It began early, with a lot of noise, cold showers, groping hands, and wooden paddles that were applied to the women's buttocks as we crawled through the corridors of the men's living quarters. Then we were led up on deck, where the heat was searing and the bright sunlight momentarily blinded us.

My roommate and I chose to be among the last to be initiated, hoping the revelers would grow tired. They didn't, and we suffered the consequences. After having gooey, thick black grease energetically rubbed through our hair and on the front of our blouses by male crew members, and spoiled food poured over us and then rubbed in, I looked over at the swimming pool. From what I was able to witness of the line of women who were far ahead of me, our last act would be to jump in. The pool—which was now filled with a dark, thick, slimy mixture of water, oil, food scraps, and floating scum—was uninviting. As I warily contemplated taking that plunge, I was pushed forward and confronted by my attacker.

He gloated as he offered me the choice of kissing him or a dead fish that had been rotting in the hot sunlight for hours. I could tell by his expression that all previous victims of the initiation had chosen to kiss him, and he had no doubt that I would follow suit. I wanted to reject him; but as I looked at and smelled the dead fish, I started to gag. Very close to vomiting, I looked up and read his surprise at my indecision. He prodded me to choose, then he grinned again. The victorious look in his eyes made me choose the fish.

He gasped in disbelief, then grabbed my head and pushed my face against the fish for several very long seconds, preventing me from breathing. When he finally released me, I looked up and realized he had been defeated. My intent was to avoid him, but I had (unknowingly) publicly humiliated him.

After that incident, he never blocked my path as I walked to class. When we accidentally (but only momentarily) came in contact with each other, his behavior was proper. Later, as I regained confidence and held my head up high, and felt safe walking alone on the ship, he treated me with courtesy. Finally an occasion arose where I had to go to his work station. Since my friends were in class, I was forced to go alone. Although his behavior toward me had changed, our meetings had all been chance occurrences, and I was nervous about appearing before him. I feared he would misconstrue my actions.

When he looked up and saw me, his expression showed surprise. He treated me in a professional manner, and I lost my fear. As our transaction neared completion, he paused, looked at me intently, tipped his head in a silent salute, smiled faintly, then completed the business. As I walked away, I was stunned. I realized the look in his eyes was one of respect.

I knew I was safe. And, just as they had been in the past, my memories were repressed, buried in my subconscious mind where they could do no harm. I suspect that if I had retained and consciously focused on them, eventually they would have triggered the memories of the childhood abuse at a time when I was not ready to cope. The memories of the shipboard molestation were buried so deep that, until recently, they were the last truly destructive memories that I have recovered.

Control Issues

Control issues are very important to survivors, and their need to maintain control is something others may have difficulty comprehending. Long after she knew the details of my abuse history, my best friend asked, "Why do you always need to be in control?" She couldn't understand that I lost control when I was molested, and that loss continued through all the years when my attacker repeatedly terrorized me. Nor could she understand that I was not in control during all the years when I experienced unexplained fears, when I felt fragmented, when I felt I was a stranger even to myself. In order to break the cycle of abuse, I had to regain control of my life.

The simple truth is, it's hard for those who have not experienced childhood sexual abuse to understand what the child experienced. It is also difficult for them to understand what adult survivors must go through in their battles toward recovery.

Control issues permeate my life. When I am in control and things are moving smoothly, I feel a heightened sense of security. Anyone can experience the need to be in control, whether or not they were sexually abused. But I think survivors are more at risk when they are not in control. The following are three examples of ways in which I have taken control.

First, I prefer to take control at work because I feel secure in knowing I can influence the outcome and ensure the job gets done properly. When the loss of a co-worker's position due to budget cuts interfered with my ability to get the job done properly, thus putting me "out of control," my health suffered until I was able to make the necessary adjustments. I also take control at work by putting myself in a leadership position, including leading several staff self-help groups. As a result, I am able to initiate things that need to be done and move the groups in what I believe are appropriate directions.

The second example of how I took control of my life illustrates the extreme to which survivors will go in order to secure their safety. After my memories began returning, I suspended my social life. Basically, I went to work and then went directly home afterward. I refused to enter settings where I might encounter the slightest risk. This control mechanism protected me, but at great cost.

Now I am beginning to occasionally venture out on my own during daylight hours. In trying to become dependent upon myself, I am experimenting with extending my boundaries. I move carefully, testing to see that I can maintain control and still be safe in these new settings. With each successful outing, I gain confidence and come closer to exploring the possibility of trying something new another day. But at this point, I am still unwilling to go out at night—even with my husband.

Finally, the most delicate situation in which I took control concerns my writing. For years I worked successfully with a coauthor. But as our lives moved in different directions, through mutual consent we dissolved the writing partnership. The changes challenged our friendship. They also forced me to hone my skills and learn to believe in myself as a writer instead of mentally connecting my success to our joint ventures. But most importantly, accepting the challenge of writing solo has allowed me to regain control over my healing tool and my recovery efforts.

There are many ways in which survivors can regain control, including the following.

- Survivors can enroll in self-defense classes to build confidence and work toward discarding fear.
- Survivors should surround themselves with a support network.
- Survivors can make decisions about positive life changes and implement them. Begin with little things that will likely end in success; later, tackle bigger issues.
- Survivors should try to avoid situations in which they will feel manipulated or where they will feel pressured to agree to compromises that they don't want to make.

Are Victims of Sex Crimes Recognizable by Perpetrators?

Once my memories of the second attack by a different man returned, I often wondered if the first man's actions influenced the second. Is it possible that victims of childhood sexual abuse, or victims of any sexual abuse, are recognizable by men and women who would attack them? By their stance, their bearing, their bowed heads, their tentative behavior, the scared look in their eyes, do survivors unintentionally send signals to those who would harm them? Can perpetrators recognize victims and know they are easy prey while the rest of humanity is unaware of their torment? Can survivors mask the terror, pain, and horror from everyone but those who would further abuse them?

The idea that people who view themselves as potential victims may indeed identify themselves to potential attackers through their body language and mannerisms is troubling, but it is supported by recent research. In publishing the results of his clinical study on the relationship between childhood sexual abuse and chronic medical problems, Vincent Felitti cautioned, "These patients often fit into multiple categories of sexual abuse and are often abused by multiple persons within any given category, suggesting that the initial event predisposes to repeated sexual trauma."[1]

This research should not be interpreted as implying that victims of sexual abuse are at fault, nor should it frighten those who were abused. It should, however, serve to keep survivors alert and cautious of how they present themselves in public. Once survivors know which traits are identified by perpetrators as "markers," they can look for these behaviors in themselves and work toward modifying or eliminating them. Knowledge can be converted to strength, power, and the ability to implement change, while ignorance can be extremely dangerous.

One important point to remember is that as survivors grow older, they do have the power to bring about change. They can implement behavior modifications. They can seek help. They can move away from the perpetrator's influence. They can work toward reclaiming control. They can speak out, adding their voices to those of other survivors. They can choose not to be victims any longer!

Suggestions for Survivors

- Try to understand childhood sexual abuse is not about sex.
- Try to understand the power exerted by the perpetrator is terribly destructive.
- Try to accept that childhood sexual abuse can affect many aspects of your life.
- Try to accept that you are not responsible for the attack.
- Try to accept that each instance of abuse is damaging.
- Try to accept that abuse by multiple perpetrators is damaging.
- Try to accept that the psychological, emotional, and spiritual abuse is damaging.
- Try to reclaim control.
- Try to gain comfort from understanding you *can* break the cycle of sexual abuse.
- Learn to think of yourself as a survivor, rather than a victim.

Suggestions for Friends and Family of Survivors

- Try to understand that childhood sexual abuse is not about sex.
- Try to understand the power exerted by the perpetrator over the survivor is terribly destructive.
- Try to understand how all-encompassing childhood sexual abuse is to the survivor.
- Try to understand that survivors don't "allow" the abuse experiences to ruin their lives.
- Try to accept that survivors are not responsible for the abuse.
- Try to understand that victims of childhood sexual abuse are doing everything they can to survive.

- Try to accept that survivors can be victims of multiple abuse occurrences as well as victims of multiple perpetrators.
- Try to understand that the abuse experiences are terribly damaging.
- Try to accept, without questioning, the survivor's need to regain control. When appropriate, assist in this process, but allow the survivor to determine the level of participation.

Conclusion

Misconception #13 is untrue. Sexual abuse is about degradation, power, fear, manipulation, and destruction of boundaries, not about sex. Rape victims who are asked to describe the worst part of the attack frequently answer, "I thought he was going to kill me."

That same terror rape victims experience ensured my silence, darkened my nights, and sent fear through my body whenever males approached me. It is the terror that convinced me that almost any man is strong enough to inflict bodily harm on me. It is the terror that still makes it very difficult for me to trust men.

Misconception #14 is based on two faulty assumptions. The first is that a single act of sexual assault on a child is no big deal and the child should easily overcome it. In fact, survivors have to learn to value themselves, to build themselves up, to trust themselves and others, to face what happened. They have to negate all the misconceptions that surround this heinous crime. And then they have to deal with the attacker, to face the fact that the perpetrator was responsible, to appropriately place the blame where it belongs. And after survivors have worked through mourning and all the other emotional issues, they have to finally accept what happened. This process can take years—or a lifetime. Some survivors never reach the point where they can begin the recovery process, others never complete it. No one who hasn't experienced it can truly understand.

The second faulty assumption is that childhood sexual abuse only happens once. Many survivors are victims of multiple attacks and often of multiple attackers. Yet survivors can change the pattern. If children know about sexual abuse—and who to blame—before it happens to them, and they have been encouraged to seek help if it does happen, perhaps they will summon the courage to tell. Adult survivors may influence the pattern by consciously changing their behavior so they exude confidence even when they don't feel in control.

Survivors of childhood sexual abuse should try to think of themselves not as victims but as survivors. A victim is weak; a survivor is strong. A victim will cower and be manipulated; a survivor will face challenges. A victim will fall prey to others' plans; a survivor will triumph. A victim gives up control to others; a survivor regains control. The image anyone projects is what others receive. If survivors project strength, they will become stronger!

I gain comfort from the fact that, as a 20-year-old victim who had no memory of being sexually molested as a child, I took steps that ended the chain of abuse. On some unconscious level, I chose to stop being a victim and become a survivor.

> *"The empowerment, it's like a ripple of water that keeps expanding and expanding. Our struggles are so tremendous as women, but our rewards keep coming in bits and pieces."*
> – Elena, a survivor, quoted from an interview by
> Margot Silk Forrest, editor, *The Healing Woman*

> *"Keep breathing. When you take a full breath you proclaim your right to live."*
> – Louise M. Wisechild
> *The Obsidian Mirror*

12

Confronting the Issue of Confrontation

*Surviving childhood sexual abuse requires one measure
of courage, while facing it later requires another.
I learned much about hidden strength when I was forced to
confront my past. Rather than continuously fighting
the truth, eventually I learned to embrace it.*

Misconception #15: Confrontations are non-threatening and
should be a part of every survivor's healing process.

In fact, confrontations—particularly those not carefully planned
or staged at the appropriate time in the healing process—can be very
damaging to survivors.

* * * * *

During my journey toward recovery from childhood sexual
abuse, I have gone through many stages. Over the last few years,
through positive private and public disclosures, I have gained self-
esteem, released the guilt, and placed the blame directly on my
attacker. I no longer accept the shame of one who has been sexually
abused. Recently, I reached the point where I began to think about
confronting the man who violated me. I knew it would be a big step
and probably a dangerous one. And yet I felt I was strong enough and
ready to take the risk. I just didn't know if I wanted to.

Because of some negative experiences with private disclosure, in
which I was blamed and disbelieved, I felt I had already experienced
some of what I would go through if I chose to confront my attacker.
I knew there was a very real possibility he would deny what had
happened, trivialize the abuse, rationalize his behavior—or blame me.

I felt strong enough to combat any negative feedback I might receive from my attacker, yet I wasn't sure I wanted to put myself at such great psychological risk. I had reverted to experiencing nightmares for a six-month period after one pressured disclosure and knew it was very likely I would undergo such a regression with confrontation. I wasn't certain I wanted to do that to myself.

Earlier, while doing research for an article I was writing on disclosure, I conducted telephone interviews with two counselors. Bobbi Hoover of Santa Clara, California,[1] a therapist who works with incest survivors, spoke about confrontation: "Move cautiously. Make sure you are one hundred and five percent ready to do it!"

I strongly believe confrontation should be a positive move for survivors, one more step to take in the healing process, one more way of regaining control of their lives. Bobbi Hoover says, "Tell what you need to tell and don't expect anything back. You are confronting for yourself, not because you expect help from him. Be healthy and strong enough so you aren't disappointed with the results of confrontation."

Therapist Kathy Duguid of Menlo Park, California,[2] who works extensively with incest survivors, cautions, "Don't consider disclosure [confrontation] until you have worked through what happened to you—until you are clear on what happened, what you feel, and the depth of the pain." I felt confident in this regard, and I also realized it was important not to be influenced by others when coming to a decision about confrontation. Some of my negative experiences with disclosure came about because I was pressured into acting before I was ready. Ms. Duguid advises, "Don't be persuaded by literature or friends/lovers/spouses.... You must have the freedom to make the decision yourself!"

Especially in the case of confrontation, it is far better to err on the side of caution. If survivors decide to delay the confrontation, they are not choosing that it will never happen. Instead, they are merely postponing it until they are certain they are ready for such a challenge.

In approaching the matter from a cautious perspective, I decided there are four things I wanted to do in any confrontation—prepare myself, protect myself, set realistic expectations, and take control of the situation.

The preparation part involves being psychologically ready for whatever happens. It is imperative that the survivor be strong when confronting her attacker. That strength serves as a protection against a possible new verbal attack. Then, if the perpetrator denies what he did, that denial won't trigger the survivor's own doubt or denial.

In protecting myself during a confrontation, I realized I would not want to go alone. Since I haven't utilized counseling as part of my healing process, I had no access to a logical source of support. I discarded the idea of putting any family member or close friend through such an ordeal, knowing they would not have the necessary detachment or training to support me in the way I might need to be supported. Therefore, I decided, if I became determined to go through with the confrontation, I would call one of the counselors I had interviewed and ask for her recommendations.

My decision is supported by Kathy Duguid, who says survivors need two or three people who are specifically chosen to help them through recovery, and who are consciously committed to their recovery for a period of time (even if only for a month). Survivors can arrange to meet such people by contacting Incest Survivors Anonymous.

After failing to set realistic expectations during private disclosures, I was determined not to make that mistake again. I decided not to expect anything positive from my attacker during confrontation. The sole purpose for such an encounter would be to express my thoughts and feelings. Kathy Duguid cautions, "Be clear on your motives. If you are hoping the perpetrator will say he is sorry, that won't happen. Be clear on what you are hoping to get out of the confrontation. Be realistic!"

Because so much of my life has been influenced or controlled by what happened to me as a child, most of the time without my knowledge, I feel it is extremely important that the survivor be in control of the confrontation scene. To me, the whole purpose for confrontation is to reclaim control.

In considering the issue of confrontation, I realized it isn't something one rushes into, nor should it take place before the survivor is well into the healing process. Kathy Duguid advises, "Do confrontations at the end of therapy, when you have worked your way through your own doubts and you know what happened." She suggests further precautions if the abuse occurred within the family: "When confronting [your] family or [a] perpetrator in [your] family, you should be in therapy. If possible, have the confrontation take place in therapy. You need safeguards to protect yourself physically ... [and] emotionally. Many families can't handle what happened. You need protection in order to handle your own emotional outpouring." Since my abuser was not a member of my family, at least I didn't have to worry about this additional, extremely stressful issue.

Finally, I believe survivors who enact confrontations need to allow a period of recuperation and rebuilding after meeting with their attackers. Setting this time aside allows survivors to assess their success with confrontation, to reassert their belief in the truth of their past, and to gather strength before moving ahead with their healing journey.

* * * * *

Before I came to a decision about confronting my attacker, I learned he is dead. At first I felt great relief that he could never harm me, or anyone else, ever again. Then I began to feel frustrated because the choice I had been agonizing over—whether or not to confront him—had been taken away. It seems that, even from the grave, he is manipulating me and controlling my life. But I don't want to grant him such power!

At last I reached the point where I began to fear my healing would stop because I was unable to confront him, and I wondered how I would resolve this issue. Many therapists suggest visiting a perpetrator's gravesite and even pounding the ground over the grave if it relieves a survivor's anxieties.

I don't know where my attacker is buried; if I did, I don't know whether or not I would go. Sometimes I lie awake at night and visualize his grave, and in my mind I enact a scene where I talk to him. I tell him what I think of him and the effect his actions had on me. I tell him how I feel about myself because of what he did to me. I scream at him, and I cry. To date, this behavior hasn't provided much relief because I don't know how he would have responded. Then I remember his taunting laughter and the look in his eyes when he threatened to kill me. And I am still afraid!

Writing a letter—but not mailing it—may serve as a source of healing when confrontation is not possible. If letter writing doesn't work, writing a poem or drawing a picture that depicts the abuse, or sending a donation to an organization that works with survivors may. California therapist Bobbi Hoover suggests "empty chair" role playing as a useful tool in allowing survivors to release their feelings.[3] Survivors can also double role play, which allows them to speak for themselves and give a perpetrator's response that satisfies them.

When survivors are well along in their healing process, they can also get involved in activities that allow them to feel good about themselves in the context of their abuse experiences. Attending or speaking at conferences on childhood sexual abuse, corresponding with other survivors, and sharing with other survivors the results obtained through using their healing tool (e.g., writing, poetry, drawings, paintings, quiltwork) are very empowering experiences.

Suggestions for Survivors

- Consider the matter of confrontation very carefully before making a decision.
- Try not to consider confronting the perpetrator until you are well along in the recovery process.
- Try not to consider confronting the perpetrator until you are secure in your own reality and know what happened to you and the consequences to you of the perpetrator's actions.
- Try not to allow your decision on confrontation to be influenced by well-meaning friends and family.
- Work on other ways to resolve your feelings if you are unable to confront your attacker.

If you decide to confront your attacker, you should:

- Plan the confrontation very carefully.
- Be prepared, particularly for a negative experience.
- Protect yourself; take someone with you who can maintain emotional distance from the confrontation.
- Set realistic expectations; don't expect to receive anything positive from the attacker.
- Do it for yourself as a means of taking back control.
- Maintain control of the confrontation.

Suggestions for Friends and Family of Survivors

- Try to understand how difficult it is for survivors to consider confrontation.
- Try not to apply pressure on survivors regarding confrontation.
- Encourage the survivor to take someone who is detached from the situation with her when confronting.
- Support the survivor's decision regarding confrontation, and be there for her before and after the matter is resolved.

Conclusion

Misconception #15 is false—confrontations can be unhealthy and/or dangerous. Undertaking confrontation when a survivor is not ready for such a scene can set him back in the healing process. As is true of so many aspects of recovery from childhood sexual abuse, confrontations carry a risk factor that is impossible to measure in advance. The prospect of further terrorization is very real to survivors.

These are just some of the reasons why determining whether to confront the perpetrator is such a difficult matter. There is much at stake in proceeding with confrontation. Survivors need to protect themselves on so many levels—physically, psychologically, and emotionally. Survivors also need to make sure they recognize the truth of the abuse so that nothing the attacker says during a confrontation will cloud their vision of what happened. Finally, they need to decide for themselves.

I have not yet come to terms with whether it matters that I can't confront my attacker, but I am frustrated that he still exerts control over me. Kathy Duguid confirms the generally held belief that a person can heal with or without confrontation. I am now trying to release my new anger and fear so I can draw comfort and understanding from her words. And I'm trying to teach myself that it doesn't matter that he took something else away from me—the option of making this final decision about confronting him. I draw strength from knowing, in the end, I am the one who survived!

"Great emergencies and crises
show us how much greater our vital resources
are than we had supposed."
– William James
*American psychologist and philosopher;*1842-1910

"Courage is the price that life exacts
for granting peace."
– Amelia Earhart

13

A Survivor's Choices

*Victims of childhood sexual abuse live through experiences
that no one would wish on his or her worst enemy.
Survivors must embrace a life that some of those who were
not abused can't talk about or even admit exists.
Our everyday reality isn't even captured in the worst
nightmares of those who do not share our understanding.
And yet, even after enduring such horrifying
conditions, we choose to live.*

Misconception #16: One day the survivor's journey
will be over.

A survivor's journey will, in fact, never be over. Often victims of childhood sexual abuse have been exposed to long-term trauma as the abuse played out over many years. As the information on recent medical studies and my own chronic health problems, presented in this book, substantiate, the end result of such long-term trauma is an altered state of being. The symptoms observed in survivors, when accurately diagnosed, are identified as Post-Traumatic Stress Disorder (PTSD). The effect is the result of psychological and physical terror inflicted upon survivors.

The psychological/emotional fragmentation that was explained earlier in this book is also common among other groups of people who were exposed to long-term trauma, such as those who survived internment in concentration camps during World War II. Those people share with sexual abuse survivors similar experiences of the loss of self. They also share with sexual abuse survivors similar experiences of terror and loss of control.

Like survivors of childhood sexual abuse, death camp survivors relied upon the mercy of their captors (abusers) for their very lives. Like survivors of childhood sexual abuse, death camp survivors display a remarkable will to live and belief in the worth of life even under the darkest circumstances.

In their book *Reclaiming Our Lives: Hope for Adult Survivors of Incest*, authors Carol Poston and Karen Lison dramatically equated the experiences of survivors of incest with those of victims of Nazi concentration camps. Both groups were forced to submit to degradation, violence, and pain, and yet were expected to exchange those experiences for life-giving ones. They wrote that incest survivors "... live with truths many 'normal' people can hardly bear to hear."[1] Faced with such a difficult task, living in a society that doesn't understand, how can the survivor's journey ever end?

* * * * *

The ability to consciously make our own choices is something most people take for granted. It is frightening to even consider the possibility that the person we will become and the life we end up leading could be determined by events we don't even remember. Yet that is exactly what happens to survivors of childhood sexual abuse. The direction their lives take is formed during a time when they may have no memory of the dark deeds that occurred in their childhood, deeds that may control parts of their lives before they begin to heal, deeds that will affect them for the rest of their lives.

During the repression stage, which often covers far more than just the formative years, most major life choices are made. I made these decisions at a time when I was haunted by nightmares filled with dark shadows; at a time when I felt splintered, frightened, and alone. My decisions were impacted by my abuse experiences.

Twelve years ago, at age 34, I began recovering my memories of being sexually abused. As I struggled with the truth, as the pieces of my past were unveiled and slowly, painfully fit into place, I began to finally understand the events of my life and the person I became. And I now understand the choices I made.

There are five areas where major life decisions were made by my subconscious self during the years the memories were repressed: sexual repression, education, career, marriage, and children. Now that the memories have returned and I have spent years attempting to heal and recover, the veil has lifted. I am finally able to understand those decisions and the effect my past has had on molding my life and my future.

Sexual Repression

As a result of the sexual molestation and my attacker's continuous terrorization over the next 12 years, I grew up sexually repressed. My fears directly affected my feelings about my body and impacted on every relationship I had with males.

Since fear became the cornerstone upon which each relationship was built, it influenced my willingness—or unwillingness—to participate in intimate situations and colored my male friends' views of me. At a time when I should have been able to take pleasure in myself, and my changing body, I hated myself. And I feared men!

When I was in college, I met a man whose religious background had instilled in him the desire to "wait until marriage." Because of his patience, for the first time I was able to relax and enjoy a relationship with a man. As the relationship flourished, I began to realize not everything connected with our bodies is bad. After the relationship ended, it was very difficult for me to find myself, once again, faced with the following choices: (1) entering relationships where I experienced fear or (2) being alone.

Education

Decisions centering around education presented the next set of choices. I desperately wanted to attain a college education, hoping that success would bolster my lack of confidence and self-esteem. I chose to pursue an education in the field of sociology with an emphasis in social psychology. Years after completing my degree, when I began my recovery efforts, I relied on instincts that were developed and honed during my college years. My education has served me well during my healing journey.

Career

Choosing a career is one of the most important decisions anyone makes, but for survivors it is especially critical to their well-being. Survivors are at risk because of their lack of confidence, low self-esteem, fear of strangers and of the unknown. And women survivors often have a terrible fear of men. If survivors are placed in the wrong situations, they can again be victimized. If they are placed in the right situations, they gain a sense of their own worth.

After working at two other full-time jobs, over 20 years ago I accepted a staff position at a university. I like being in a setting where the end product is knowledge instead of profit. I am surrounded by a group of people who care about one another and who are very giving human beings.

Now that I understand the truth about my past, I realize how important the work setting has been to my survival. It is a place where I am able to utilize my education, serve others, and thrive. It is a place where I am respected and where I feel safe. It is a place where I meet decent people who share my interests; many of them have become my friends. In the comfort of such an environment, I feel secure. Drawing on the strength of this support network, I was able to accept the challenge of healing when the time came.

Marriage

Marriage is a key issue for all survivors of childhood sexual abuse. How can they learn to trust anyone of the opposite sex enough to feel safe in making a life-long commitment, especially if they don't remember what happened to them or know why they feel tormented, afraid, fragmented? And yet they desperately want these close relationships to verify their worth as human beings.

Because of the conflicts that rage within them, many survivors choose not to marry. Others marry and have disastrous relationships. Others find happiness through their marriage. Still others fall somewhere along the happy/unhappy continuum in committed relationships that do not culminate in marriage. For each survivor there is a different story. But survivors who successfully commit to a partner can attest to the uniqueness of the mate who accepts the challenge of such a relationship. And they gain strength and a sense of self-worth when their partners willingly continue to assume the burden of living with the aftermath of childhood sexual abuse.

Survivors are haunted by many things as they decide whether or not to marry. There is the blank part of their lives, the part they don't understand or even remember. They also don't understand why they can't trust. When I faced this decision, society stubbornly expected men to be the "breadwinners," yet I was afraid of being financially dependent upon any man. For me, there is always fear of strangers, fear of intimacy, fear of excruciating pain during physical contact. Survivors may feel these are unreasonable fears, but again they don't understand.

In choosing my life partner, I selected someone I felt comfortable with, someone I could talk to, someone I believed understood me even more than I understood myself. From the moment we met, I trusted him. That feeling was unusual because, like so many other survivors, trusting any man had always been (and continues to be) a major problem for me. I chose to marry a man whom I would have described as my "best friend." I chose a man who accepted that I must be financially independent of him. And, without understanding the importance, I chose a man who has a physical disability. It is unlikely he could physically harm me. Because I chose not to be sexually active before marriage, I also didn't understand the problems we would be forced to face after marriage.

When my memories began returning 12 years after we were married, finally I began to understand why I am the person I am. And at last I understood the torment I felt during intimate/sexual situations. With that knowledge came tremendous guilt because of the things I denied my husband, and what I feared I might always be forced to deny him. With that knowledge came anger because the actions of my attacker have robbed me of the ability to share completely in sexual situations. But my husband's patience and understanding, and willingness to undergo what must be tremendous physical strain in order to grant me the time I need to work through this issue, have gained him my undying admiration and appreciation.

His first words after I blurted out in shock the truth of what had happened to me were, "Now I understand." His calm acceptance of the truth, and his willingness to accept me as I am, gave me the time to find the strength and courage to begin the journey toward healing. He is, truly, a participant in my recovery, and he has experienced his own agony. He has consciously chosen to be my ally; he has suffered for me, with me, and because of me. The men and women who choose to stay with those who were sexually abused as children are courageous, giving, self-denying, and they, too, become survivors!

Because most sexual assaults on children occur at the hands of a perpetrator of the opposite sex, many survivors are uncomfortable with relationships involving members of the opposite sex. Although I believe gender choice is, for the most part, inborn, I suspect in a small number of cases people do choose their sexual preference. Bobbi Hoover of Santa Clara, California, a therapist who works with incest survivors, supports this theory: "My experience is that gay men 'knew' early on they were 'different,' as do some lesbians I know. Other women, I believe, did make the choice to be with women." [2]

If indeed some survivors do choose their sexual orientation, I suspect one key factor in making the decision to enter a same-sex relationship may be a history of having been sexually abused as children. Their choice concerning sexual preference helped alleviate their fears; it also provides a means of adapting and coming to terms with their history of childhood sexual abuse, perhaps resulting in their leading happier and healthier lives.

Entering a relationship with a same-sex partner, whether by choice or because the gender identity was inborn, offers a degree of protection, but it certainly doesn't solve the problems created by the sexual abuse nor does it bring about a speedy recovery. These same-sex couples must work through the same intimacy, fear, trust, betrayal, hurt, safety, guilt, shame, and other issues that heterosexual couples face. They have the added difficulty of working through their problems in a highly homophobic society.

The problems all couples face are compounded when a survivor is involved because these relationships do not include equal partners. This may sound cruel, but one partner—the survivor—should be allowed to determine the amount of participation he will accept from the mate during recovery. The survivor should decide whether the partner will participate fully, partially, or not at all.

It isn't an easy choice for the survivor, and I'm sure it's not easy for the partner either, particularly if the two want different things. The survivor might want full participation from her mate while the mate feels uncomfortable with the whole issue of childhood sexual abuse and would prefer that the survivor deal with it alone. Or the survivor might want to shut the partner out while the partner wishes to actively participate in the recovery process.

It's a tough position to be in! In order to ensure her own well-being, the survivor must maintain control over the situation. In order to protect the relationship, the partner must go along with things he may disagree with. It takes a lot of hard work and understanding to be the partner of a survivor!

I also feel strongly that a survivor's partner should know about the abuse at the earliest possible moment. I'm not advocating forced disclosure, nor am I suggesting telling someone on a first date. But if the relationship is becoming serious, the survivor has recovered the memories, has begun to deal with them, and feels strong enough, the truth should be told. No relationship can thrive while there are such monumental secrets.

There is risk involved in confiding to a partner. But if the partner is incapable of dealing with the history of abuse, and ultimately wants out of the relationship, I feel it is better to know sooner than later.

If a survivor is in a committed relationship when the memories begin returning, again I feel strongly that the partner should be told as soon as possible. Relationships are complicated enough without having the added pressure of one partner withholding the truth about something so traumatic as a history of childhood sexual abuse. Even when the facts are not known, the abuse experience is bound to have an impact on the relationship. Survivors can hide the truth, but not the fallout from their past.

Therapist Bobbi Hoover invites the partners of her clients to attend an "educational session" with her. This allows them to learn the facts about sexual abuse in a non-emotional manner in a non-threatening setting. It also allows them to ask questions and receive answers. Further, it provides support for the many difficulties involved in maintaining the union and for the seemingly overwhelming problems they must face if they remain in the relationship.

My husband was with me when my memories began returning. In shock, I confided in him without realizing I did so. If it hadn't happened that way, I don't know how I would have found the strength to tell him, or when I would have determined the time was "right." I just know it was essential that he understand.

Since that time, I have discussed my past with him whenever I felt the need to or whenever I wanted to reassure myself that he was handling the situation. Occasionally I need to know that it's okay with him that I still can't participate in intercourse (especially since we engaged in what was, for me, very strained and tormented intercourse in the early years of our marriage).

Throughout the years of my healing journey, I have chosen, for the most part, to undertake my recovery alone. Maybe making that decision was possible because of the emotional support I received from my husband. Perhaps if he hadn't been so accepting I would have felt the need to include him more often, to try to "make him understand."

But no matter what level of involvement a survivor chooses to request or accept from his partner, there are ways the two can share intimate moments that will impact on the recovery process without directly focusing on the history of the abuse. The keys to success are moving slowly, not forcing anything, and displaying patience, understanding, and love.

Survivors and their partners must overcome many problems related to the childhood abuse experiences, but I think the most difficult to deal with are sex-related. These are the issues with which I have had the least success. Part of the problem stems from the way healing occurs. Initially, I had to deal with the physical/body elements of the abuse. Then I had to address the psychological, emotional, and spiritual issues.

Now I must, again, work on physical/body (sexual) issues. I, wanted to believe they were resolved! It seems like I have to turn the clock back and focus on elements that I previously addressed. That feels a lot like failure. Yet it isn't! In fact, I'm now faced with addressing a very different set of physical/body issues—ones that don't just involve me. And that is part of the problem. For years, I chose to exclude my husband from much of my recovery process. Now I must focus on an area that very much involves him.

Consciously recognizing I have problems with sexual matters is a giant step forward. Many survivors have trouble admitting sexual problems exist, or they like to believe they are handling the sexual issues. Occasionally survivors convince themselves that they have resolved their sexual problems when, in fact, they haven't. These problems have to be identified before they can be solved.

Therapist Bobbi Hoover says, "... it is my experience that dealing with incest/molest is like peeling a very large onion and so often the actual part at the very center is physical/sexual intimacy."

It is important that survivors and their partners understand why the sexual problems are so difficult to resolve. Survivors know, on a rational level, the person they are now involved with and committed to is not the perpetrator. Survivors don't understand why they feel such pain and terror when they are with someone they love.

The problem is that the same body parts that were abused in childhood are the ones involved in the physical expression of adult love. It is very difficult for survivors to separate the past from the present, particularly if intimate settings trigger flashbacks that involve reliving the abuse.

As the survivor becomes more comfortable, and experiences how satisfying it is to physically share, he or she will become more willing to experiment with bodily stimulation. Eventually the survivor will learn to understand the power of physical sharing between two people who love each other. Finally the survivor may learn how empowering these types of non-threatening experiences can be.

One important measure of a survivor's progress toward recovery is the ability to regain control over his body. Being able to enjoy the physical aspects of his life indicates the survivor has taken back something the perpetrator stole so long ago. Being able to physically share with another is a true indicator that healing has progressed because the survivor is choosing to share that part of his being that has been reclaimed.

Children

Childbearing can be a difficult issue for anyone; but for survivors of sexual abuse, it can be grueling. Survivors who are still repressing the memories live with numerous unexplained fears. They constantly display conflicting behaviors which they can't explain. They have difficulty making decisions, are plagued with self-doubt, feel unworthy of being loved, and have problems with sexual situations. These are not ideal conditions under which to explore the possibility of parenthood.

Survivors who have recovered some of their memories can understand many of the things that were mysterious about their lives, but they are faced with a whole new set of problems. How can they get beyond the hurt, betrayal, and difficulties with intimacy? And how will their past affect their interaction with their own children? In short, will they be good parents?

During the years I was repressing my memories, my husband and I postponed making a decision about having children. The time never seemed right. There were too many things that got in the way. When I thought I wanted to have children, my husband wasn't ready; and when he was ready, I wasn't.

When I turned 35, one year after I began retrieving my memories of being sexually abused, we finally had to come to a decision about having children. I was just beginning to face the truth of my past, and I felt incapable of doing more than simply coping with my current reality. I chose not to have children, but my husband and I agreed that we will adopt if the time ever comes when it is right for us to become parents.

At the time, I didn't realize how much my past influenced that decision. Now I am beginning to comprehend. Although I have never regretted making this decision—I still feel the risk was too high when considered in the context of my need to recover and heal—I am fully aware of the price I have paid. I love children. As I get older, I realize how much the actions of the man who attacked me have continuously played a role in my life. Choosing what was necessary to secure my health and well-being robbed my husband and me of many wonderful memories. But even more, it robbed us of the chance to love and be loved by a child.

Suggestions for Survivors

- Try to understand that the abuse experience will always be a part of your life.
- Try to recognize and honor the choices you have made.
- Try to understand many of the choices you made were impacted by the sexual abuse experiences.
- Try to understand that many of the choices you made were dictated by the need to feel "safe."
- Learn to think of yourself as a survivor, rather than as a victim.
- Try not to give up control of your life to the abuse experience; recognize the ways in which you have survived.
- Try to recognize the good that has come from the choices (conscious or unconscious) you have made.
- Try to accept and love yourself.
- Try to accept your limitations.
- Try to accept the affection and caring your mate offers.
- Try to celebrate the person you have become.

Suggestions for Friends and Family of Survivors

- Try to understand the abuse experiences will always be a part of survivors' lives.
- Try to understand that the choices made by survivors are influenced by their abuse experiences.
- Try to understand that participating in a relationship that involves a survivor will be challenging as well as frustrating.
- Seek professional help in order to learn to understand what is involved in participating in a relationship with a survivor.
- Learn everything you can about childhood sexual abuse.
- Try to accept the survivor's limitations (including those regarding trust and honesty).
- Try not to place demands on the survivor.
- Try to be patient, understanding, caring, loving.
- Allow the survivor to dictate the parameters of the relationship.
- Allow time to work through the sexual issues if you are the partner of a survivor.
- Allow the survivor to dictate the parameters for involvement in the recovery process.

Conclusion

I have grown tremendously during my recovery, enough to know my journey will never be over. I have come to look upon the growth process as being similar to the grieving process experienced after the death of a loved one. The vestiges of sorrow will remain but in time, as healing occurs, they will become a part of the background instead of remaining in the foreground.

I have come far enough in my healing journey to know I can't erase what happened to me, and at last I accept it. During the repression stage, I unconsciously made decisions that allowed me to live through the ordeal that haunted my youth and formed me into the woman I was at age 34. During the recovery process, through learning to acknowledge the truth, I became the woman I am at age 46. By facing my past, I am taking command of the direction my life will take with full knowledge of where I have been. And now, on a conscious level, I am making decisions that will help me move toward the next stage of recovery. Through taking up my pen and disclosing the truth, I am consciously participating in the process of molding the woman I will become.

Although my attacker took many things away from me, he did not deprive me of the ability to choose. The most important choices I made were to survive and to heal!

> " *Human free will is basic. It takes precedence*
> *over healing. Even God cannot heal a person who*
> *does not want to be healed.*"
>
> – M. Scott Peck
> *People of the Lie*

> "*You can't let your heart go bad like that, like sour milk.*
> *There's always a chance you'll want to use it later.*"
>
> – Barbara Kingsolver
> *Animal Dreams*

14

My Body, My Self

For most of my life, I tried to contain the hurt to my body.
That action resulted in my being unable to experience
deep emotions, and it created a new and different kind of pain.
Now that I have allowed my emotions to surface,
I feel like the finger has been removed from a
leaky dike and I am about to drown.

Misconception #17: The only harm done during sexual abuse is physical; once the body heals, the child heals.

Although the physical damage is bad enough, there is also psychological, emotional, and spiritual damage that must be healed after any sexual assault, especially after a sexual assault on a child. The depth to which survivors are damaged in a non-physical manner when childhood sexual abuse occurs is unmistakable.

* * * * *

One night, about 24 years ago, while I was in college and still living at my parents' home, I was sitting at the desk in my bedroom studying for a test. Suddenly I looked down at myself from a corner of the room near the ceiling. I didn't know what had happened to me, but I saw what could only be described as my empty shell—my body—bent over the desk. It didn't move; there was no sign of life. I watched, not understanding. I was in a realm that seemed to have no restrictions, no physical sensations; it made no sense. I didn't know how or why I entered that strange state, but I had the distinct feeling the part looking down on the shell was the real me.

I had entered a very different world. I couldn't touch, hear, smell, or feel in the usual sense of these words. Yet I could see everything in a whole new way that offered understanding of a different level and dimension. There was no pain or fear; there was quiet, calm, peace. I don't think I remained in that altered state very long. Suddenly I was aware of the division in my being and I became consumed with the most dreadful fear that I couldn't get back into the shell. The moment panic surfaced, I was back in my body.

Once I knew I was safe, I thought about what had happened, and I didn't understand. I hadn't tried to do whatever it was that had occurred to me, and I couldn't explain it even to myself. Although the ordeal was over, it was frightening to me—an unknown, an experience over which I had no control. I didn't tell anyone. It seemed too incredible to be believed, so I refused to think about it. I simply put it out of my mind.

Without realizing it, that solution was a small part of a larger pattern I had used for almost 10 years to avoid remembering, thinking about, or dealing with unpleasant things. It was a pattern that began when I was sexually molested during childhood. As the terrorization continued over the next 12 years, each time my attacker left my parents' house, I buried the hurt, fear, guilt, and shame deep in my subconscious mind. Since I was unable to deal with it, it was best not to remember it.

* * * * *

I didn't recall the paranormal incident until about 10 years after it happened. As my husband read aloud to me from a book about out-of-body experiences, I gasped. At last I had a name to call it and words to describe what had happened to me. I felt safe talking with him about it. There was no fear that I wouldn't be believed. He was amazed and intrigued as he listened, particularly since he had never experienced anything like it himself. Although I still didn't know how it happened, and I didn't care to explore the matter further, there was relief in telling what I had experienced.

After the discussion with my husband, I again forgot about the out-of-body experience. However, a few years later I began recovering the memories of my childhood sexual abuse. As I began waging the long and lonely struggle for survival that has consumed most of my energy, called upon all of my capabilities, and forced me to change in ways that at the time were unimaginable, I have gained a great deal of comfort from remembering that paranormal experience.

Although I still don't understand how it happened, I have developed an explanation for why. As I remembered the experience, I realized, although I had entered a realm apart from what we know in this world, I was still me. I retained my thoughts, beliefs, and awareness; but I wasn't confined to my body. In losing many of my senses and all feeling, I was released, free, and yet in touch with the universe around me. And I suspected the realm I entered was a better one because I had shed the confines of my body.

I now look upon the out-of-body experience as preparing me for the ordeal that lay ahead of me when my memories began returning. It helped me deal with the pain and uncertainty. It exposed me to a living world where there was no pain. And it showed me that the body and the essence of the person—the spirit—are two separate things. Physically leaving my body allowed me to understand this world and to gain some knowledge of the next one. Experiencing physical separation from my body later provided one key to dealing with my history of childhood sexual abuse.

I was able to understand that the mind, or spirit, is separate from the body, but lives within it. Thus, it followed that the attack on my body could be contained there. He didn't attack me, he attacked my body. When the memories became too painful, I was able to mentally separate my self from my body. Thus, I was able to reduce the infliction of pain on "me."

It was so easy to perfect the separation process, once I became consciously aware of the abuse, that I realized it was something I had long been doing—in high school, college, and throughout my adult years. In both high school and college literature classes, I was always one of the top students. And yet, through those classes, I left signs (if anyone had known to look for them) that I had problems with sexual issues.

In high school, my teacher wrote the following critique on a book review of *Gone With the Wind*: "This is an 'A' paper except that you treated this book as if it were only a war story. What about the romance between Rhett and Scarlett? Grade: B-Plus." My college literature professor wrote the following on a paper discussing *Jane Eyre*: "This should have been an 'A' paper. Your study of character development is beautifully written. Why did you ignore the romantic relationship between Jane and Mr. Rochester? Grade: B-Plus." The process my teachers noticed but did not understand is called "literary disassociation."

I remember a comment made by a friend in college—that all the guys thought I was asexual. He didn't say it in a hurtful way, although it did hurt; he just stated a fact. My male friends had noticed something different about my behavior, something unusual in the way I interacted with them, something that set me apart from our female friends. They noticed my unwillingness to allow my body to be a part of me. Twelve years into my adult journey toward healing, I now have the words to describe it: To me, my body is only the vessel that houses my essence, my spirit; it doesn't count!

The body/spirit separation that occurs in my mind has successfully allowed me to deal with my childhood sexual abuse. It has served as a tool in my healing process. But it has caused tremendous physical damage because, through this separation process, I was unable to feel physical pain or to experience my emotions.

I didn't begin to realize how severe the damage was—or the cause of it—until I read an article by survivor Margaret Matthews in which she said, "... I began to realize that when I cut off at the head, I didn't have access to the bodily resources I needed to fully recover my rage or fear...." [1]

Prior to reading her article, I felt the separation of my mind and body was a good thing. Now I realize physical and emotional separation cannot take place over a long period of time without causing extensive damage. After reading Ms. Mathews thoughts on the need to nurture oneself and live in harmony with one's body, I realize how little I took care of myself and how out of harmony I was.

Ms. Matthews offered the key to my understanding in her concluding sentence, "I must notice the pain in both my mind and my body, acknowledge it and give it love." With my newly-achieved understanding came the realization that I allowed the hurt inflicted by my attacker to continue, unchecked. I allowed my attacker to take even more from me—the present. By discounting the body, I discounted that the hurt went beyond the body. He didn't just attack my body, he attacked me—all of me! I ignored that my "being" is one system composed of body, mind, emotions, and spirit.

By ignoring my body, I gave up a portion of myself to him, saying it didn't matter. And I believed he did nothing to my mind. In fact, that's where most of the damage lies. He robbed me of my innocence, joy, trust, security, pride, self-esteem. And he robbed me of the mental pleasures that are connected with my self and my body.

After reading Margaret Matthews' article, I have spent considerable time assessing the differences in the way we each approached our healing and realizing that what she wrote is true. Finally, I realize that she is farther along in the healing process. Further, through recognizing the value of the lesson she taught and attempting to alter my approach to my mind/body separation, I realized how important the input of other survivors is to the recovery journey. After implementing changes, I am now much healthier.

In September 1992, while watching a movie on television titled "Go Toward the Light," I gained a deeper understanding. The movie, which was based on fact, centered around a couple's struggle to prepare their young son, who had AIDS, for death. When the father finally accepted that his son would die, he poignantly told the boy about life and death by demonstrating with a glove. As he put his hand into the glove, he spoke about the spirit living inside the body. As he removed his hand from the glove and cast it aside, he talked about the spirit leaving the body and living on, even after the body dies.

While watching that demonstration, suddenly I realized, in order to survive the shock of reclaiming the memories of my childhood sexual abuse, I had to separate my spirit from my body. I had to lessen the pain, to buy time, to cope, to gain strength. That process allowed me to make it through the first 12 years of my recovery. Having finally accepted what happened, I must now find a way to reunite my spirit with my body. Doing so will allow me to continue to heal and go on living. The final separation of the two entities should come only with death.

Suggestions for Survivors

- Try to understand the damage inflicted was not just physical.
- Try to accept that during the initial years of recovery you may have needed to separate your mind from your body in order to survive.
- Try not to question your sanity if you experience strange occurrences (e.g., paranormal experiences).
- Try to accept that the extraordinary experiences given to you are gifts that can serve as tools in recovery.
- Try to recognize the psychological, emotional, and spiritual damage inflicted, then work on healing it.
- If you separated your mind from your body, you should try to re-integrate these elements. This could involve meditation, exercise, or developing an artistic talent (e.g., writing, painting).

Suggestions for Friends and Family of Survivors

- Try to understand the damage inflicted was not just physical.
- Try to understand that the internal damage may be even more difficult to heal than the physical.
- Try to understand that any bizarre behavior displayed by a survivor is part of his attempt to survive.
- Try to accept that paranormal experiences may be a part of survivors' coping and recovery efforts.
- Support the survivor.
- Try not to place unreasonable expectations on the survivor.
- Throw away your mental measuring stick for "normal" behavior and accept the survivor as she is.
- Try not to rush the survivor or pressure him to heal.
- Try not to demand complete recovery.

Conclusion

Far more than physical damage occurs when a child is sexually abused. In dealing with the physical damage, it is not advisable to continue to separate the mind from the body over a long period of time. Many survivors do use this technique as a tool in surviving and later in working toward recovery. Eventually however, this severing extracts a tremendous toll on the quality of the survivor's health and life.

Once survivors have begun to work through the physical issues, they must integrate their minds and bodies and begin working on the psychological, emotional, and spiritual damage. I have found that healing the inner damage is even harder than dealing with the physical damage (with the exception of sexual issues). In facing these inner conflicts, survivors can no longer deny the pain that was inflicted. They must rebuild from the inside out.

I have learned many lessons throughout my recovery journey, including that there are many ways in which survivors must heal. And the healing is easier if survivors remember they are not alone. A common background as survivors of childhood sexual abuse binds survivors together in a way that is irrevocable. Without choosing it, survivors must walk along a similar path. Through sharing, the path becomes a little smoother, the distance still to travel a little shorter.

As survivors take each step along the healing journey, others who have gone before them are there to teach them and to share their pain. That sharing allows survivors to understand themselves, thus diminishing the pain. That display of support encourages survivors to continue walking along the path toward recovery. Eventually survivors will learn to smile, and then to laugh again, as others who share their experiences cheer them on!

"One does not become enlightened by imagining figures of light, but by making the darkness conscious."

– Carl Jung

"As you remember fragments, you're grasping for the facts. But you know what you feel. That's real. Recovery is totally about feelings."

– Elena, a survivor, quoted from an interview by Margot Silk Forrest, editor, *The Healing Woman*

15

It's Not Just About Me Anymore

*Just as a stone tossed into still water causes ripples
through a pond, childhood sexual abuse impacts on the lives of
those closest to the victim. For most of my life, I tried
to contain the hurt within myself. Recently, I have come
to understand that action denied the hurt inflicted on others.
I now know the effects are even felt **years**
after the physical abuse has ended.*

Misconception #18: Childhood sexual abuse
only affects the child.

This is far from the truth. It impacts upon the lives of mates, parents, brothers and sisters, friends. In fact, whether they know it or not, it affects everyone close to the survivor. The closer the relationship, the more the person will be touched by another's history of abuse. This chapter demonstrates how far reaching the effects of childhood sexual abuse can be on those who are close to survivors but who were not, themselves, abused.

* * * * *

One evening as my husband and I were preparing to go to bed, he began talking about the writing project I was working on—incorporating reviewer suggestions into this manuscript. It is unusual for him to bring up the subject of my abuse; he almost always waits for me to indicate that I wish to discuss it. As we talked, I realized we hadn't engaged in such a conversation in quite some time. During the first few years after my memories returned, we discussed it much more frequently than we have in the last few years, probably because initially I needed to know he was handling the situation. After those early conversations, I was mostly silent on the subject as I became consumed with my own struggle to recover and eventually to heal.

That night, he talked about the ways I have changed since we first met, especially in the years since my memories returned. He said he has watched what I've gone through in dealing with the facts of my abuse, and he has seen the toll it has taken on me. He has seen my lows and highs as well as my weakness turning into strength. He talked about seeing my terror as the most devastating memories returned. He spoke about how recovering my memories changed my behavior. And he talked about watching me learn to live with my past and my present, and how I was slowly overcoming the past.

Then, very sadly, he said he still really can't understand what survivors experience. Not even after being married to me for 23 years; not even after watching my all-consuming struggle to recover. No matter how hard he tries, or how much he wishes to share in that knowledge, it is not to be.

He paused a moment, and I understood his pain. I could tell he felt helpless in assisting me, and he believed he had let me down. He then mentioned that after watching what I have gone through in dealing with my returning memories and my reality, he does know how very difficult it is for survivors to make it through each day.

Again he paused and I heard his unspoken anguish and his frustration that he couldn't offer more. Yet he offered exactly what I needed. He remained calm when the memories returned and, in shock, I blurted out the truth to him; he accepted my past. He listened when I needed to talk, he allowed me to be silent when I wasn't able to share, and he backed away when I needed space. Because he recognized the truth of my life struggle, he refrained from voicing unrealistic expectations. And when I needed his understanding, he was always there for me—no matter how bizarre the circumstances, no matter how unrealistic my fears might have seemed. His support made me feel comfortable with myself, despite my limitations. His acceptance has been a key to my ability to undertake healing.

I told him some of the ways I felt he had been supportive over the years. And then I said I hadn't expected him to understand what I'd gone through as a child, but that I was pleased he had been able to understand what I was going through as an adult.

He seemed relieved to know he had played a positive role in my healing. At the end of the conversation he expressed his tremendous admiration and respect for the courage I have displayed in undertaking my recovery and in making it through each day.

As the discussion drew to a close, I realized his words touched on something that had been bothering me while writing this manuscript. In Chapter 11, "Breaking the Cycle of Sexual Abuse," I wrote: "The simple truth is, it's hard for those who have not experienced childhood sexual abuse to understand what the child experienced." That belief is expressed several times throughout this book; however, I was writing from my instincts, not from my experience. Although the literature in the field substantiates my belief, I was still uncomfortable with making such an assertion. Now I had my husband's testimony to back up my words! In fact, our discussion helped me realize none of us can ever truly understand what another is experiencing.

That night, I had trouble sleeping. The conversation stirred something deep inside me, and I felt a great deal of disquiet. His words made me focus on the early years of our relationship, and I realized the tremendous toll my struggle had taken on him. In Chapter 13, "A Survivor's Choices," I wrote: "The men and women who choose to stay with those who were sexually abused as children are courageous, giving, self-denying, and they, too, become survivors!" As I thought back in time, I realized just how true those words are.

There are two areas in which I underwent major behavioral changes over the years of our marriage that directly impacted on my husband. The first concerns my sexual behavior and the second involves my behavior in non-sexual situations.

Sexual Behavior

In the early years of our marriage, my husband and I engaged in intercourse on a very irregular basis. It was painful for me to deny him the physical side of marital sharing. It was equally difficult for him to listen to me say I wanted to have sex, then watch me move away from him in fear as he approached. My words communicated one thing; the look in my eyes and my bodily responses said something entirely different. Intimate settings triggered tremendous fear—fear that I couldn't understand or explain to my husband. As time passed, we had sex even less frequently.

It wasn't until 12 years into our marriage that we finally understood the reason for my fear. After my memories returned, during sexual situations, I experienced flashbacks of the attack. At last we agreed it was better to participate in intimate moments that did not include attempting intercourse. That way, the experiences would be positive and enjoyable ones. We have learned there are many ways to show our love—sharing, holding, touching, talking—without participating in intercourse.

Like many survivors, I don't know when (or if) I will be able to resume normal sexual relations with my husband.

Behavior in Non-Sexual Situations

When we got married in 1970, we were both going to college. Living in the San Francisco Bay Area, we had easy access to an assortment of wonderful things to do. During those early years, we spent most evenings in coffee shops drinking tea and studying. On weekends, we drove to Berkeley to browse in bookstores or sit and read in one of its many unique restaurants. We also spent time with other young couples. We regularly drove to San Francisco or took a picnic lunch to the beach. We participated in "fun runs" that were sponsored throughout the area. Occasionally, we went dancing or to private parties given by our closest friends. Although I was always uncomfortable, shy, and introverted when I was among large groups of people, I survived these ordeals because my husband was nearby.

When my memories of being sexually abused returned, my life changed drastically. My husband's also changed. I was no longer willing to go out at night. I was no longer comfortable with social interaction, even in daylight. The most he could get me to do was take a drive on the weekends—and I remained in the car. My refusal to follow our long-standing patterns forced him to choose from among two options. He could either stay home with me (which was unfair because he is self-employed and spends the weekdays at home alone), or he could go out alone.

Without a doubt, the development of my ability to cope with everyday situations slowed with the recovery of my abuse memories. My reclusive behavior over the last 12 years has taken a toll on my husband, yet he has never complained or criticized. In fact, he has been supportive. He has somehow understood and silently accepted that the changes ensured my daily survival.

There are probably thousands of times when he watched me do things that were bizarre, and yet he expressed no disapproval. Sometimes he asked about my changed behavior, attempting to understand. When I began walking on the portion of sidewalk nearest the street, he asked why. I replied that I felt safer that way. The cars presented less threat than men who could approach me from the buildings. He noticed when I became more introverted, walking hunched over, my gaze trained on the ground. He watched as I became nervous and averted my eyes in fear as men approached me. He accepted when I became unable to make decisions or adapt to change. And he silently accepted when I continuously refused to go out at night.

The following two incidents stand out in my mind as times when my husband instinctively knew what I needed.

* * * * *

One summer afternoon several years ago, my husband and I were gardening in our back yard. Suddenly I became very quiet and he asked what was wrong. I replied that I found a dead bird. He offered to bury the bird, but I insisted on taking care of it myself. I got the shovel and walked toward the bird; but several feet away, I froze. He noticed what had happened and asked if I wanted help. I replied that I would handle it, but my body would not follow my brain's commands. My feet would not move, and I started shaking violently.

He came over to me, took the shovel, and buried the bird. Then, he again came over to me and hugged me until I stopped shaking. When I regained my sense of calm, I was embarrassed; I feared I had behaved like a child. He told me it was all right, that I didn't have to try to force myself to do something I wasn't capable of doing. I never forgot that incident or his kindness in understanding my limitations. In fact, he understood better than I did. Until he accepted me, I couldn't accept myself.

* * * * *

By the time several years passed after my memories returned, I had gone through many of the beginning stages survivors experience. Among these stages were attempts to suppress, then denial, guilt, shame, fear, and pain. One evening, my husband and I were still in bed after sharing some intimate moments. Suddenly my body was gripped by a terrible feeling. I sat up, enraged at my attacker. I started crying and then screaming at him. I lost control as I rocked back and forth, sobbing between bursts of swearing fits. At last all the pent-up emotions were coming out in a frightening display of cleansing.

Having never seen such an outburst from me, my husband asked if I was all right. I just continued rocking, crying, and screaming. He asked if he could help, if I wanted him to hold me. I shook my head; there was nothing he could do. He stayed near me, watching as the rage continued to spew out of me.

Finally, I got up, went to the bathroom to get several tissues, then returned to the bedroom. The crying continued, only now it came in loud jerks and gasps and sobs. I didn't think it would ever end. Nor did I believe the pain in my heart would ever go away.

Eventually my anger escalated to the point where I felt I couldn't contain it, and I feared I would explode. I screamed that the bastard had no right to touch me, to invade my body, to take everything from me. I listed all my grievances concerning what he had done to me, and the way his attack had made me feel. I swore in a way I never do, from the depths of my soul. I damned him to hell as I clenched my fists. I heard the venom in my voice and was shocked. But I couldn't stop the outpouring of rage, nor could I alter the course it was taking. And that was good. The poison that had been dammed up inside me had been injuring me for over 30 years. Finally it was being released.

At long last the rage was spent, and I was left with an intense ache unlike anything I have ever experienced. I continued to rock back and forth, but now I wailed—for my loss, for the things that had been taken from me so long ago, for the person who died the moment he launched his vicious attack. And I mourned the birth of the child, teenager, young adult, and mature adult the attack molded me into.

This went on for an extended period of time, and all the while I was conscious of my husband's concern. He followed my directive to leave me alone, but he remained by my side. He was silent, watching in case he could be of assistance, not touching me.

Finally my emotions were spent and I collapsed onto the bed, exhausted. I was wrapped in the silence that now engulfed the room, and I felt drained. The rage was gone, but I felt empty. And lonely. And hurt. And in pain.

My husband asked if I was all right, and I said yes. He asked if I wanted him to touch me, and again I said yes. He took me into his arms and held me against his chest. For the longest time he silently stroked my hair and my back. Comforted by his closeness, concern, acceptance, and love, eventually I fell asleep.

* * * * *

The evening my husband brought up the issue of my history of sexual abuse, I lay in bed thinking about the sacrifices he has made over the years we have been together. I particularly thought about the sacrifices that were required because of decisions I have made. I became overwhelmed with his willingness to accept what I needed in order to survive. Good marriages are supposed to be based on mutual input and joint decision-making, and yet often such sharing is impossible in unions that include survivors. Whenever their welfare and peace of mind are at stake, survivors act—often unconsciously—to protect themselves.

Over the 24 years of our marriage, there have probably been thousands of times when things I did, either consciously or unconsciously, forced him into situations that were beyond his control and may not have been what he would have chosen. There have also been a number of times when I made major decisions that impacted on my husband's life, such as having an abortion and choosing not to have children.

Although I thought about the effects these decisions would have on my husband, I had to make them based upon my own well-being. We discussed the situations and he accepted my choices. And never, in all the years since the decisions were made, has he given any indication he resented that I made the choices, nor has he ever said or done anything that would show lack of support for the decisions I made.

I am deeply grateful for his willingness to be a part of the world that is my life. I admire and respect him for allowing me to set limits that should have been reached by mutual agreement, and for choosing to remain by my side even after he began to understand what that loyalty would require of him.

Suggestions for Survivors

- Try to understand that your abuse experiences will affect those who are close to you.
- Seek to discover the ways in which you have changed.
- Try to accept that you may be different from others.
- Try not to punish yourself for the demands you make on your partner.
- Allow time to work through sexual issues.
- Try to remember your partner has chosen to be with you.
- Release your emotions whenever you can; doing so helps release the poison that has been held inside for so long.
- Acknowledge how special your partner is.
- Listen to and try to learn from the positive comments made by friends and family.

Suggestions for Friends and Family of Survivors

As your relationship with the survivor grows stronger, you will probably continue to be shocked and outraged by what happened to the person you care about, and you may want to help. And as the survivor's behavior forces you to make changes that you might not choose, you will feel the strain of coping with the fallout from the sexual abuse. But it is important for you to remember your actions and expectations will directly impact on the survivor's ability to heal. It is vital that friends and family become a positive force in the survivor's life. For that reason, again I am providing additional details about some of the following suggestions.

- Try to understand the abuse experience will always be a part of the survivor's life.
- Try to understand that participating in a relationship that involves a survivor will be challenging as well as frustrating.
- Try to understand that survivors' abuse experiences *will* affect them.
- Always allow the survivor to set the guidelines for your involvement in the recovery process. Friends and family have no way of knowing what the survivor is going through. He may be experiencing nightmares, recovering new memories, regretting having disclosed. Friends and family should let the survivor indicate when he is ready to move ahead and further include others in the recovery process.
- If possible, seek professional help.

Suggestions for Partners of Survivors:

- Learn everything you can about childhood sexual abuse.
- Try not to place unreasonable demands or judgments on your partner/survivor. Doing so will diminish her already battered self-esteem.
- Try to understand how difficult it is for your partner/survivor to get through each day.
- Try to accept your partner/survivor's limitations (including those regarding trust and honesty).
- Try to be patient, understanding, caring, loving.
- Try to recognize and celebrate the fact that this person that you care for *is surviving.*
- Always allow the survivor to set the guidelines for your involvement in the recovery process. You may not know where your partner/survivor is in her healing. Let her indicate when she is ready to move ahead and further include you in the recovery process.
- Partners should allow time to work through the sexual issues. If survivors ask their partners to go to counseling, they should do it without being embarrassed. Many men and women who

were sexually abused as children experience sexual problems before the memories return. After the memories start returning, survivors frequently suffer from flashbacks when they are in sexual situations—even though they know their lover is not the attacker. Partners should be prepared for a lengthy wait before any return to their usual lovemaking practices, as well as for the possibility that lovemaking may never return to what it once was. This is not an easy problem to work through. It will take time, patience, understanding, and a lot of self-denial.

- Expect and accept setbacks in the survivor's recovery. Even after survivors move toward recovery, there will be times when they will revert to old behavior patterns. When the moments of self-doubt strike, you shouldn't expect more from your partner/survivor. Remember, she is doing everything she can to heal.
- Offer support and encouragement to your partner/survivor, but don't negate her feelings. Many survivors think they are ugly, and this psychological picture is very real to them. Listen, accept your partner/survivor's descriptions, then talk about what she sees. Tell her she is courageous, talented, attractive. Also, discuss the ways in which she has changed. Words of acceptance will help to improve her sense of worthiness and self-esteem and reinforce that she is moving in the right direction.
- Allow your partner/survivor as much "space" as he needs (this may entail being alone much of the time).
- Try not to put your partner/survivor in threatening positions.
- Learn to interpret the survivor's body language.
- Try to remember, no matter how frustrated you feel, it is far worse for your partner/survivor.
- Talk to your partner/survivor when he indicates a willingness to discuss the issue of childhood sexual abuse.
- Tell your partner/survivor how special she is and how much your relationship together means to you.
- Try to understand that bizarre behaviors on the part of the survivor are part of his attempt to survive.
- Throw away your mental measuring stick for "normal" behavior and accept the survivor as he is. Regular standards of behavior do not apply to survivors. Even "normal" behavior for a survivor doesn't always apply. On good days, I feel like I can do just about anything. On bad days, I have difficulty placing

a phone call or crossing the street. I have learned to live with these inconsistencies—at least now I understand them.

- Try not to rush your partner/survivor or apply pressure by setting timetables for recovery. Survivors must move forward at their own pace. Pushing will contribute to their feelings of self-doubt and low self-esteem. And it can frighten survivors. It may also add to their failures if they take steps (to please others) that they are unprepared for. Also, try not to make comparisons with others. Let survivors heal in the ways they can in the time they need.
- Try to be aware of any time your partner/survivor makes any type of improvement, comment on it, and celebrate it. No matter how small, any improvement is a victory!
- Try not to demand complete recovery. Some survivors will fully recover while others may attain only partial recovery. Remember, any amount of recovery is a positive step.
- If possible, seek professional help.

Professionals can help you learn to understand what is involved in participating in a relationship with a survivor. Although I am fortunate that my husband accepts my past and listens when my pain emerges, not every partner can or will react in such a supportive manner. Many partners feel threatened when they learn about the abuse. They may react with confusion or rage, wanting to "get the S.O.B.!" However, this type of reaction is destructive.

Through seeking professional help, partners can learn to identify their true feelings about the history of abuse and determine whether or not they are capable of providing support to a survivor. If the partner is not able to do so, it's best to find out as quickly as possible. If these partners remain with the survivor, the relationship becomes burdened with their unspoken anguish.

These suggestions will not always be easy to follow. One key to success is to offer support and encouragement but not expectations. Remember, an incest survivor is a wounded soul in the process of healing. Only the survivor has the power and right to determine the course the healing will take. It may be that any particular survivor may have only enough strength to survive. With luck and your support, recovery may also be possible.

For men and women who endured childhood sexual abuse, surviving is an act of strength and courage. Some days, just getting out of bed takes an enormous amount of energy. Facing and accepting the past, learning to trust, disclosing the truth, and attempting to heal put them at great risk. However, with a lot of hard work, survivors can begin to heal. When interacting with survivors, friends and family should remember the one they love is succeeding as long as he or she is surviving.

Conclusion

Only after spending years working on my recovery have I been able to focus on the ways in which my history of childhood sexual abuse has affected those closest to me. In recognizing the truth, I have been forced to confront the painful realization that the relationships I have with others are tainted by my inability to trust, to freely express myself, to knock down the barriers I erected in order to survive. These are issues that I must address in the future as I try to regain those things that most people take for granted in their interactions with others.

In particular, my history of abuse has deeply affected my husband. Often he has been forced to choose between participating in my isolated world or striking out on his own—alone. Often he has been lonely because, although we were in the same room, mentally I was a million miles away.

My husband has constantly had to put up with my conflicting emotions, irritability, and irrational behavior. And at times he has had to cope with my depression. He describes my depression states as so intense that he feels they drain his life force from his body.

Twelve years into my recovery journey, I have come a long way toward healing. I have struggled alone; and I have struggled with the support of my husband, family, and a network of close friends. I have grown stronger, but only within the context of my very protected world. And I realize there is still a long road ahead of me, for my past will always be a part of me. I have come to accept the person I am at each stage of the healing journey. I am now trying to accept the things I have asked of my husband, knowing what my demands cost him.

At last I have reached the point where I am able to look beyond my own situation when discussing the issue of childhood sexual abuse. In Chapter 9, "Breaking Silence," I wrote: "It's not just about me anymore, and I think that's a giant step forward." Only recently have I come to fully understand those words.

One of the next steps in my recovery is to work on the issues that will again open my life up to my husband. I must try to recapture a part of the woman I was at the beginning of our marriage, so we can be together in ways we used to share. I must work on the sexual issues, so our intimate moments are more fulfilling. I must focus on our marriage as a joint venture so we can thrive together, instead of continuing to focus on my individual needs and forcing us to survive in our own separate worlds. In short, I must move beyond my abuse experiences without discounting them.

I don't fool myself by thinking these changes can be accomplished overnight. Nothing about healing can be achieved quickly, or without struggle, or without pain. But recognizing the ways in which I now need to grow is the first step toward achieving these goals. If I can attain them, we will both be rewarded for my efforts. If I fail, we will continue to live apart and isolated, enduring an existence that is impoverished compared to the world that should be ours to claim.

> *"No thing great is created suddenly,*
> *any more than a bunch of grapes or a fig.*
> *If you tell me that you desire a fig,*
> *I answer you that there must be time.*
> *Let it first blossom, then bear fruit, then ripen."*
> – Epictetus, ancient Greek philosopher

> *"When you share your joy, you double it. When you*
> *share your pain, you halve it."*
> – Hungarian proverb

16

Who Will Protect the Children?

*Every man and woman **can** make a difference. The
world would still exist without Thomas Jefferson's
writings, Michelangelo's art, Mozart's music, Eleanor
Roosevelt's vision, Helen Keller's teaching, Rosa
Parks' courage. But it would be a very different place.*

Misconception #19: We are spending too much time and energy
on this issue when few children are actually sexually abused.

Nothing could be farther from the truth. Twelve years ago, when
I first began recovering memories of being sexually abused as a child,
it was believed that one in seven women of my generation suffered
such a fate. Today it is believed that one in three were so traumatized,
and it is estimated that one in five to seven men are victims of
childhood sexual abuse. Since misconceptions still cloud this issue,
apparently, as a society, we are not spending enough time and energy
on understanding the truth or correcting the problem. And, change is
coming all too slowly!

* * * * *

Before I was sexually abused as a child over 35 years ago, I had
not been taught to be cautious around family members or friends. Such
terrible deeds were only associated with strangers who moved beside
children in cars and lured them with candy. There were no television
programs that warned against or analyzed the tragedy of being abused
by someone you care for. Children were not taught what to do when
a loved one harms them. Nor were they taught that it wasn't their fault;
or that they weren't horrible, scarred, and ugly after it happened.

Children who were sexually abused suffered silently and alone. They carried the burden of securing their fragile worlds, of being responsible for their own continued existence, of protecting their families. During childhood, they assumed burdens that rightfully belonged to adults. They were no longer young.

For those abused children who buried the memories of their past in their subconscious mind, no matter how perfectly they mastered the techniques that ensured their survival, nothing prepares them for the shock and horror of the memories returning. And they will return! When mine started coming back at age 34, I truly learned the meaning of being alone.

As a society, we have come a long way since those dark days in recognizing the frequency of occurrences and the variety of dangers to children. And yet we have not even begun to scratch the surface of our responsibility to protect the children. We still want to believe such terrible things don't happen. We become bored with, or even angry about, repeated efforts to inform.

Several reasons can be offered for society's reluctance to respond to issues involving psychological trauma. First is the dilemma that, while perpetrators demand nothing (which answers society's wish to remain ignorant and uninvolved), victims require that society share the pain and offer assistance (which requires acknowledging this awful crime).

There is also the inability on the part of those who were not abused to understand and deal with what survivors go through. This is evidenced by such things as laws that allow those who are accused of sexually molesting children to be released on bail; laws that allow short prison terms for convictions in child sexual abuse cases; the lack of a reliable system for the tracking of convicted child sexual abuse offenders and provisions to keep them from working in positions that put them in regular contact with children; the reluctance of the court system to *require* court-supervised psychiatric support for all children who are believed to have been sexually abused, thus protecting the children while they come to terms with the truth about their abuse, rather than allowing them to be unduly influenced by adult caregivers—often involved in the abuse or otherwise concerned with keeping the truth silent.

Although changes are coming—slowly, far too many children are being abused while the structures of society adapt to the needed change. Despite the flood of new information available on childhood sexual abuse, misconceptions like those discussed in this book persist.

Often both society in general and the legal system in particular fail to take into account that survivors are the innocent victims of the crime.

Society's inability to understand is also evidenced by the outrage others feel about survivors speaking out and helping each other. Many people would prefer that society be allowed to operate under a "conspiracy of silence" which allows falsehoods to flourish.

Finally, as a society, we want to believe this awful deed doesn't really have any long-lasting effects. Thus, those who were not abused place unrealistic expectations on survivors. They still do not know what survivors need from them. It is still up to the survivor to take care of him or herself in this hostile environment.

Because of the existing conditions, I have had the persistent feeling that the Congressional Medal of Honor should be verbally "presented" to every survivor. "Possessing" it would give survivors something to hold onto as they learn to live with the truth of the dreadful things that happened to them—a truth they did not choose, but one they cannot escape, and one that will impact on every important aspect of their lives.

However, changes in attitudes and procedures are beginning to bring about tangible change as a result of some recent, highly-publicized cases.

In one such case, Eileen Franklin-Lipsker brought charges against her father for the 1969 rape and bludgeoning death of her 8-year-old childhood friend. During the trial, this woman gave startling testimony about how, for 20 years, she repressed memories of the dark deeds because her father sexually and physically abused her during childhood, and he had threatened to kill her if she told anyone what she had witnessed. This case got a tremendous amount of publicity and exposed the public to a first-hand account of the nightmare existence survivors must endure. Ms. Franklin-Lipsker's story was validated by the courts when her father was subsequently convicted of murder.

Similarly, over the last several years, adults who were abused during childhood by people in positions of authority (e.g. priests, ministers, teachers, coaches) have filed charges against their abusers. Investigations into such charges frequently uncovered evidence that institutions employing these abusers have historically mishandled abuse charges against authoritarian figures working for them. Several such cases have resulted in multiple convictions. The resulting publicity has forced major institutions to reevaluate their procedures for dealing with this issue, and parents have become far less willing to blindly trust the safety of their children to adults in positions once held to be unquestioningly trustworthy.

In California, Ellie Nesler was convicted in 1993 of killing the man who was accused of molesting her son and three other boys. The case raised public consciousness to a new level when it was discovered that the accused abuser had previously been convicted in 1983 of child molestation and accused in 1989 of seven felony counts of lewd acts involving four boys ages 6 to 8. The man disappeared after being released on bail. After his capture, Ms. Nesler killed him when he was being arraigned for trial on charges of molesting her son.

This case raised valid questions about why convicted sex offenders serve so little prison time, and why accused sex offenders are allowed out on bail.

In addition, a number of celebrity figures have recently come forward with their own histories of childhood sexual abuse. Their disclosures have raised public awareness while helping survivors understand themselves and their fragmented lives. With each new exposure, the likelihood that real change will come improves.

The importance of this recent exposure and the resulting dialogue is made painfully clear by considering the Clarence Thomas/Anita Hill hearings, which took place prior to most of the cases just mentioned.

During the hearings, my gaze was practically riveted to my television set. I became alarmed, then angry, then saddened as I came to realize that the proceedings were an indictment of our political system and the attitudes that still prevail regarding all sexual abuse. The questions that were being asked and the mistruths that were allowed to stand unchallenged paved the way for a disastrous ending—and I offer no opinion regarding Thomas' subsequent confirmation to the Supreme Court.

These hearings provided a test of our political structure, and it failed miserably. Once the decision was made to "go public," the Senate Judiciary Committee owed the American people the chance to understand and to learn the truth—if not about Hill's charges, then about the issue of sexual harassment. If these men weren't willing to seek the truth about sexual abuse in a case concerning adults, who will protect the children?

During the hearings, like most Americans, I was torn. When I watched Thomas, I saw a man who was outraged that he had been unfairly accused. When I watched Hill, my gut feeling told me she knew what it was to be sexually abused; she behaved with dignity and growing determination in the face of adversity.

Now that the fervor is over, I think back on the gloom that settled over me during these hearings. I realized that ugly process confirmed what I have always believed to be true—those who have not been sexually abused can't truly understand. And in this instance they didn't try to understand because, as a society, we have continuously attempted to sweep matters concerning sexual abuse under the carpet. We didn't want to know about it in the past. We didn't want to learn about it during these hearings. And some of us don't want to hear about it in the future—ever!

In thinking about Hill's behavior, and comparing it to that of abused children, I found many parallels. Among them are the following:

- Initially, she remained silent to protect herself.
- She couldn't allow the world that provided her security to collapse.
- She trusted only a few people (including a man she barely knew) with her secret.
- When she was able to move out of the sphere of influence, she set up a new life and repressed the memories.
- When she appeared before the committee and spoke in a confused manner, questions were raised about the credibility of her testimony. However, people who have survived sexual assault tend to tell their stories in a highly emotional, often contradictory, and fragmented manner that tends to undermine their credibility. It may be that, because she was at last allowing herself to focus on the horror of her past, additional memories began returning in bits and pieces during the hearings.

The above traits are displayed by children who have been sexually assaulted. They are also displayed by men and women who have been sexually abused as adults. In Hill's behavior, I saw myself at the time my memories returned and I began to uncover the truth of my past. I watched as she hesitantly recovered more memories, and saw myself. I watched as she dealt with the horror as the most difficult memories returned, and saw myself. I watched her struggle to put into words the unthinkable things that happened to her, and saw myself. I watched her painful attempt to deal with the shame, and saw myself. I watched as she faced the contempt of some members of the committee. When she didn't waiver in her belief in herself or in what she knew to be true, I saw myself. I watched as she refuted all attempts to place blame on her, and saw my stronger self.

I watched as she stood alone against the mighty power that is the U.S. government. When she didn't bow under crushing attempts to defeat her, I saw strength and courage that I wished I could claim as my own.

I have chosen to include in this book a discussion of these hearings because childhood sexual abuse and adult sexual harassment and abuse are related. The hearings demonstrated just how far some of our most respected politicians are from accepting that sexual abuse happens. Whether or not Thomas was guilty is not the issue.

Once the decision was made to hold the hearings in a public forum, the Senate Judiciary Committee should have sought the truth about sexual harassment. Instead, they gave us a sad display of how *not* to address the issue. Despite their protests to the contrary, many members of the committee displayed ignorance about the issue of sexual abuse; yet these same men write the laws that supposedly protect men, women, and children from such abuse. I kept wondering, if not these elected officials, who will protect the members of our society from such vicious crimes? Who will protect the children?

Over and over during these hearings, our leaders bowed to society's preconceived notions, often allowing fiction to be presented as fact. Among other things, the following faulty conclusions could be drawn from the hearings:

- Men and women whose public lives are exemplary can't possibly inflict such harm in private.
- The jobs men and women hold are the most important indicators of who they are and encourage or prevent them from engaging in such sick acts.
- Those who come forward with such accusations are in the wrong.

Of equally great disservice was the committee's unwillingness to allow experts in the field to testify about the behavior of survivors of sexual abuse. By barring them from appearing, some extremely disturbing testimony—from women who have no personal experience with sexual abuse—went unchecked. If experts had been invited to speak, we would have heard about the conflicting behaviors and patterns that are visible in survivors' lives. We would have learned society's expectations are unrealistic. But most importantly, we would have been warned that no one has the right to judge or try to determine appropriate behavior for survivors.

In refusing to listen to experts, the committee prevented us from hearing how survivors act and react within their own safety zones. We didn't learn how survivors set their own limits, and choose their own paths, based on the strength each possesses at the moment of assault.

We didn't hear the reasons why some survivors choose to remain in positions that put them at risk, or how fragile survivors are, or how important stability is to their well-being—even if, through maintaining stability, they must come in contact with their abuser. By blocking expert testimony, the committee prevented us from glimpsing through the window on the world that is occupied only by survivors.

The committee's actions demonstrated that we are still a country governed by men who don't understand this issue, a country governed, in part, by those committee members who chose not to try to understand or initiate change. They didn't offer the country a chance to determine the truth; they precluded it! What came through loud and clear was that these men—our chosen leaders—accepted what they wanted to believe. By accepting a man's right to pursue whatever sexual pleasures he chooses in private (e.g., enjoying pornographic material), while at the same time trashing Hill's private life, they condoned a double standard that women have long been fighting.

I was deeply worried about the effect these hearings would have on future attitudes toward sexual abuse. But my fears were relieved after the outpouring of concern became apparent. The hearing scenario horrified men and women alike. Once women began speaking out about their experiences and feelings, men began asking questions that displayed a true desire to learn. In the end, the shame I felt over the committee's behavior turned to triumph as the country rallied in an attempt to correct itself. Despite the committee's willful miscarriage of justice, many chose to become informed and to try to change.

In the time since the Thomas/Hill hearings concluded, much has changed in our perception of sexual abuse, in large part due to the number of people who have spoken out publicly and/or filed charges against their perpetrators. Although in the past those who were the victims of sexual crimes felt raped again by the system, this situation *is* changing. Although it is *still* difficult for survivors to find the courage to press criminal charges, more frequently those who do are being vindicated through knowing victory.

Most recently, some survivors are filing civil suits in an attempt to win a financial settlement for their pain and suffering. Although it is rare for perpetrators to admit to their crimes, some of their victims do win in court.

Unfortunately, in the opinion of many who are connected with outreach on the issue of childhood sexual abuse, *these* are often the cases that stimulate controversy over the issue of "false memory."

As with so many issues confronting survivors of childhood sexual abuse, determining whether or not to press charges is difficult. It involves a lot of soul-searching, self-testing, and anguish. It entails taking two steps forward and knowing there will, inevitably, come a time when they must take a step or two back. But just as there are therapists and other professionals in the field who can provide much-needed support, there are compassionate and knowledgeable people in the legal profession who have worked for years advocating for abused children and adult survivors. As these courageous people face these tough decisions, they can know others have gone before them and they are not alone.

Finally, parts of our society have begun to listen and to attempt to understand childhood sexual abuse. They have begun to realize that some men and women choose to harass while no one chooses to be harassed. That is a beginning. But it is only the first step in making those who were deaf to this issue begin to listen. My hope is that, as a nation, we will continue to make progress on the issue of sexual harassment while at the same time preparing ourselves to take the next major steps. Those next steps involve protecting the children and attempting to understand the men and women who were sexually abused as children.

Suggestions for Survivors

- Learn everything you can about childhood sexual abuse.
- Accept help from other survivors and professionals, particularly during the initial years of recovery.
- Think of yourself as a survivor, rather than as a victim.
- As you grow stronger, work toward educating others about childhood sexual abuse; doing so will help dispel the misconceptions.
- As you grow stronger, add your voice to the voices of others who are speaking out and encouraging change on issues concerning all forms of sexual abuse.
- As you grow stronger, work toward helping others who were sexually abused; it's an empowering experience.
- If possible, work toward protecting the children through becoming politically active.
- As you grow stronger, cast aside the negative mental images and think of yourself as courageous.
- Celebrate your growth, recovery, and healing.

Suggestions for Friends and Family of Survivors

- Learn everything you can about childhood sexual abuse.
- Try to understand the difficulty survivors face in overcoming their history of abuse.
- Work toward dispelling the misconceptions about childhood sexual abuse.
- Add your voices to the voices of others who are speaking out and encouraging change on issues concerning all forms of sexual abuse.
- Work toward protecting the children through becoming politically active.
- Celebrate the courage, growth, recovery, and healing of survivors.

Conclusion

After watching the Thomas/Hill hearings, I realized how ignorant our society still is regarding sexual abuse. I concluded we have not spent nearly enough time on this topic. After witnessing the dialogue that began following those hearings, and the ways that dialogue has changed—incorporating additional sexual abuse issues such as the impoverished quality of life after exposure to long-term trauma—after hearing testimony from recent court cases, I believe that necessary steps are beginning to be taken. I am encouraged that survivors are continuing to speak out, and some of those who have not been sexually abused are beginning to listen.

Until we reach the state where society provides full support for survivors, expanding their "safe" world, survivors of childhood sexual abuse are helping each other. As the broken pieces of survivors' lives fit into place—as we gain strength from our healing and our numbers—we are reaching out, building a network with other survivors. We are forming a circle around our brothers and sisters who are just beginning to face the truth of their past. We must offer comfort to one another because the world has not yet fully embraced us.

As this circle grows stronger, those of us forming it are speaking out, privately and publicly, with a united voice. This voice carries a message of understanding, acceptance, hope, healing, and love. This voice speaks with such authority that it will not be silenced. This voice is promoting new laws that will protect the children and punish the perpetrators. As this voice becomes more insistent, as it reaches out to those who were not sexually abused, it will be heard! And then there will be further change.

Watching those who form this circle, survivors find role models for their future selves. From listening to the raised voices, survivors learn how to proceed with their own recovery. Through recognizing their accomplishments, survivors will find the courage to undertake their own healing journey. Those survivors who become strong enough will join the circle and work toward making the world safe for today's and tomorrow's children. And then they will discover a different, and equally rewarding, type of healing.

> *"Healing is a lot of work and a lot of pain. But if you're not healing, life is a lot of work and a lot of pain."*
> – College-age survivor

> *"Children represent thirty percent of our population and one hundred percent of our future."*
> – Anonymous

Afterword

I can't imagine a hell worse than the existence
shared by victims of childhood sexual abuse. The fact
that we lived proves to me that there is a soul.

I had very different relationships with my grandmothers, mostly because of distance. I was close to my father's parents because we saw them frequently, while I rarely saw my mother's family because we lived in different states. But I think I was viewed as special by both of my grandmothers because in each case I was their oldest granddaughter. And I suspect there was a strong bond of expectation on my maternal grandmother's part concerning my family role because I am the daughter of her oldest daughter. She believed in the matriarch holding the family together.

My grandmothers' lives drew to a close at important times in my life, and I have always had the feeling that the moments at which they died had something to do with my life passages. I have long believed that when people are nearing death, they gain an insight into things that happened in this life as well as an understanding of all things pertaining to death and the mysteries of the universe. Some of my beliefs are supported by what happened with my grandmothers.

Shortly before moving out of my parents' home, I met the man who would become my husband. My paternal grandmother met him only once. Some time afterward, he confided in me that when they said goodbye she whispered, "Take care of my granddaughter."

I think he was as surprised as I was by her words. I had always strived to be independent, and I never thought of myself as needing to be taken care of—particularly not by a man. He and I had never even discussed marriage. And because of his physical limitations, he probably had never viewed himself as assuming the role of "taking care of " any woman.

I have always believed that near the end of my paternal grandmother's life, she clung to this world because of me. Shortly after meeting the man I would eventually marry, she died. And after her death, although I did not know what she said to him, I felt she was finally able to let herself go to the other world because she believed I would be taken care of. She sensed that I had met the man I would spend my life with. And she believed it was essential that I meet a particular kind of man, one whose positive qualities and sensitivities matched those she saw in my future husband.

It wasn't until many years later, near the time of my maternal grandmother's death, that I began to understand why it was important to my father's mother that she live to meet the man who would become my partner. I did not understand until long after my memories of being sexually abused began returning. Now that I know I moved out of my parents' home in order to escape my attacker, I suspect my paternal grandmother finally felt she could leave this world because she knew I was safe at last.

* * * * *

My maternal grandmother also met my husband only once, after we were married. Sometime thereafter, she began fighting the disease that would eventually take her life. As it turned out, that meeting with my husband was the last time I saw her alive. In Chapter 7, "Understanding My Inconsistencies," I briefly discussed some of my paranormal experiences. The following is what happened when I received a visitation from my dead grandmother.

One night when I was asleep, I had what appeared to be a dream. But I knew I was not dreaming; I knew what I was "seeing" in my sleep was real. A figure dressed in a long, green, shimmering robe with a large hood hovered at the foot of our bed. Although I couldn't see the face because the hood was pulled down over it, I knew she was my maternal grandmother. And, although at that time I had never read about such things, I also knew she was visiting me from the world of the dead. I didn't understand how she could be with me or why it was happening, but the room was filled with calm and peace. I was not afraid.

She was silent as she watched me for a long time. Finally she spoke to me through some sort of telepathy. She said, "I love you, and now I understand. I know everything. You are going to be all right. Everything is going to turn out all right. You will survive." She repeated the message several times. At last, she moved toward me; she didn't walk, it was more like she floated. She extended her hand, as if to touch me before she left. But instead of doing so, suddenly she began moving away from me.

Her retreat happened very quickly. In what seemed like only a second or two, the distance between us grew and she shrank in size. It was as if she entered another dimension because she was very far away—much farther away than the wall of our bedroom, and yet I could still see her. I could also see the wall on either side of what appeared to be a tunnel through which she was disappearing. She got smaller and smaller as she was whisked farther away from me. When she was so small that I could not see her shape, she appeared as a shimmering green light. Finally the light became so tiny that it blinked out, and the wall was solid again.

Still asleep, I wondered why she hadn't touched me and why she left so quickly. Those questions plagued me when, the following morning, I received the telephone call that confirmed she had died.

I kept the visitation secret because I was just beginning to try to deal with my recently-returning memories of being sexually abused as a child. I understood my grandmother's message, but I wasn't capable of sharing it with others.

It wasn't until many years later, while watching a movie on television with my husband, that I learned the answers to my questions. The movie explored the possibility of returning to earth after death, and it made me recall what I had observed during my grandmother's visitation. I mentioned to my husband that I thought the movie was surprisingly realistic, and suddenly he became very still. I could tell he was bothered by my comment. When I asked what was wrong, he answered, "I'm not sure I should tell you. I don't want to upset you."

After receiving my assurance that I wanted to know, he told me about witnessing something in our bedroom one night years earlier while I was asleep. He described in perfect detail what I had seen in my sleep the night my grandmother "visited." I was shocked because he even mentioned the color of the gown, which could not have been suggested by our black-and-white television set. He described how the figure had finally moved toward me, reaching out to touch me, and then quickly retreated, growing smaller and eventually blinking out. He also described the "tunnel" phenomenon through which the light was visible far beyond our bedroom wall.

I was stunned but quickly recovered. When I asked why he had not told me what he had seen, he responded that he knew the figure was from the world of the dead and he was afraid that knowledge would upset me.

I assured him that I was not upset, and then asked if he knew why the figure had not touched me. Chills went up and down my spine as he answered, "I called out to stop it and put my arm across your body to protect you." When I asked why he had reacted in that manner, he responded, "Because I was afraid the figure had come to take you away."

At last I knew why my grandmother had not touched me as she said goodbye. I didn't tell my husband what I knew about the events of that night because the pain of my recovery effort still enveloped me. But I kept clinging to my maternal grandmother's words, trying to believe I would find the strength to accept and then move forward with my healing.

* * * * *

As I look back on what I have had to deal with in trying to recover from the physical, psychological, emotional, and spiritual abuse that took place in my childhood at the hands of a man who was supposed to be a family friend, I know all survivors of sexual abuse must go through a similar hell. Because of the actions of their attackers, survivors are stripped of those traits which normally make up humanity. They must exist in a different realm and build upon a different reality.

Child survivors have to create a new identity that encompasses the abuse experiences, even if they don't remember them. They live, despite the torment they have to face. Adult survivors who are attempting to recover must create a new personality that embraces and eventually, through recovery and healing, goes beyond the abuse experiences. In doing so, they live in a related but different hell than the one that enveloped their childhood.

The hell that is the early stages of recovery, when an adult survivor has to stop denying and face the full truth, is such a painful and tormenting process that it cannot possibly be described. During these years, adult survivors must face their worst nightmares and they must answer the question, "Why didn't I die?" At times the pain is so great that they wish they had died. And yet they continue to live, developing an inner strength that often they do not recognize. While fighting bouts of depression, they must reaffirm their will to live. They must respect and honor the commitment they made as a child to cling to life. They must discover the depth of their resources to endure.

Survivors who are just beginning to retrieve their memories, or who have just begun their recovery journey—particularly those who experienced death threats at the hands of their attackers—should gain strength from reading the words of author Terrence Des Pres. In his book, *The Survivor: An Anatomy of Life in the Death Camps*, Des Pres explains that, because they feel "... closer to death, survivors are rooted more urgently in life than most of us. Their will to survive is one with the thrust of life itself, a strength beyond hope.... In this state a strange exultation fills the soul, a sense of being equal to the worst. And as long as they live, survivors *are* equal to the worst." [1]

During this tremendous struggle to cope and continue to live, adult survivors of childhood sexual abuse must come to terms with their feelings about their souls. During the darkest hours, they may feel that their soul died at the time of the assault, that only their outer shell survived. This feeling stems from the horrible internal damage that is inflicted during such an attack. As adults survivors attempt to recover, they must recognize that their soul lived and is the powerful force behind their survival. The soul provides the incredible inner strength that keeps survivors going, that makes their lives worth living—despite the horror and degradation. The soul provides the strength that prevents abusers from winning in the end.

As survivors of childhood sexual abuse move toward healing, they must willfully cast aside the psychological terror of bearing an imaginary "scarlet letter." That image should be replaced with a mental "red badge of courage," representing the inner strength all survivors must discover within themselves if they hope to move toward recovery. They must find the courage to seek out the truth instead of pushing it away. They must begin to accept the past in order to be free to embrace their whole self. Only then will survivors be able to reach deep within themselves to find the courage to heal.

As survivors grow stronger, as they treat their pain, honor their rage, and learn to move ahead with their lives, they begin to focus more on getting through each day, instead of on why they didn't die. Eventually survivors who strive for recovery reach a point in healing where their abuse experiences are just a part of their life experiences, not the major focus. They no longer try to deny what happened to them; instead, they pour energy into changing the things they can change. They no longer ask why they didn't die. These survivors celebrate life, and the fact they have survived.

* * * * *

During the years since my grandmothers' deaths, I have drawn comfort from the fact that, in those moments before they died, they understood as no one else close to me can. I believe, through some awakening that comes just before death, they were able to share my memories, to feel my pain, to understand what it would take for me to cope with life. And after this knowledge became a part of them, they found ways of letting me know they accompany me on my journey.

I have used the comfort I gained from their messages during my recovery. With their encouragement, eventually I came to understand that my soul survived the attacks, and that all parts of my being could live through the reclaiming and healing processes. Their words helped me search for the vast reserves of strength that I feared I didn't possess. Their messages bolstered me during the moments of greatest pain and deepest depression, and eased my feelings of loneliness and rejection.

With the help of my husband, family and special friends, I have found the courage to try to heal. At the end of 12 years of recovery efforts, I know the battle is far from over, and I accept that I may never come to the end of my journey. But I have made tremendous progress, and I now accept myself as I am. This acceptance frees me to continue the journey. At last I have reached the point where I can again experience joy. I am glad I am alive.

If my grandmothers could send a message to me today, I think it would be that they are proud of me and they will be with me as I continue the journey toward recovery. I hope they know that their messages were received, have been a source of comfort, and have had a major impact on my ability to heal.

Because of my repressed memories and nightmares, initially I existed in the dark tunnel that encompasses many survivors. Bolstered by my grandmothers' messages, when I was strong enough, I was able to turn on the inner light and make the darkness disappear. And that inner light will continue to warm me and shine on my pathway to recovery and healing, no matter how long it takes.

At long last I can say with joy and pride, I have survived! That is everything.

The truth has become my shield.
It has been tested by the fires of my private war,
and it has turned to steel.
It will protect me for all eternity.

Endnotes

Chapter 4: Returning Memories: Real or Imagined?

[1]   John Briere, Ph.D. is Associate Professor of Psychiatry at the University of Southern California School of Medicine. Judith Herman, M.D. is Associate Clinical Professor of Psychiatry at Harvard Medical School, and Director of Training at the Victims of Violence Program in the Department of Psychiatry at Cambridge Hospital, Cambridge, Massachusetts. Both graciously granted permission for material contained in their May 26, 1993 position papers, presented to the Annual Meeting of the American Psychiatric Association at a forum titled "Adult Memories of Childhood Trauma: Current Controversies," to be used in this book. For purposes of this discussion, references from these papers are indicated by parenthetical notations of the appropriate clinician's name, followed by the appropriate page in the position paper where references can be located; e.g. *(Briere, page #); (Herman, page #).*

[2]   Linda Meyer Williams, Ph.D. is a Research Associate Professor at the University of New Hampshire Family Research Laboratory, a Senior Research Associate at Joseph J. Peters Institute in Philadelphia, Pennsylvania, and a member of the Executive Committee of the American Professional Society on the Abuse of Children. Material from her Summer 1992 article "Adult Memories of Childhood Abuse: Preliminary Findings from a Longitudinal Study," appearing in *The Advisor* is included in this section. References to this article are indicated by the following parenthetical notation of her name, followed by the appropriate page number of this issue of *The Advisor*; e.g. *(Williams, page #).*

Chapter 5: Turning Self-Punishment into a Positive Part of Survival

[1]   Carol Poston and Karen Lison, *Reclaiming Our Lives: Hope for Adult Survivors of Incest* (Boston: Little, Brown and Company, 1990), 251. **Reprinted by permission of the publisher.**

[2]   This information was written by incest survivor and therapist Barrie Ann Mason in an article titled "Incest, Anger, and Spirituality," which appeared in the September 1992 issue of *The Healing Woman*.

Chapter 7: Understanding My Inconsistencies

[1]   Vincent J. Felitti, M.D. is head of the Department of Preventive Medicine at Kaiser Permanente in San Diego, California. He has done a number of studies on chronic illness among survivors of childhood sexual abuse. Information from those studies, which appeared in *Southern Medical Journal* in March 1991 and July 1993, was used in this discussion. References to the two articles used are indicated as follows:

"Long-term Medical Consequences of Incest, Rape, and Molestation," *Southern Medical Journal*, Vol. 84, No. 3, March 1991, pp. 328-331. References within the text appear as *(Felitti-1991, #)* indicating the appropriate page number in this volume of *Southern Medical Journal.*

"Childhood Sexual Abuse, Depression, and Family Dysfunction in Adult Obese Patients: A Case Control Study," *Southern Medical Journal*, Vol. 86, No. 7, July 1993, pp. 732-736. References within the text appear as *(Felitti-1993, #)* indicating the appropriate page number in this volume of *Southern Medical Journal.*

Chapter 9: Breaking Silence

[1]   Kathy Duguid, M.A. is a Licensed Marriage, Family, Child Counselor practicing in Menlo Park, California. She kindly granted author Elizabeth Adams a telephone interview during which they discussed disclosure and confrontation issues regarding recovery from childhood sexual abuse. References to information obtained during this conversation are directly credited to Ms. Duguid in this text.

[2]   Bobbi Hoover, M.A. is a Licensed Marriage, Family, Child Counselor practicing in Santa Clara, California. She kindly granted author Elizabeth Adams a telephone interview during which they discussed disclosure and confrontation issues regarding recovery from childhood sexual abuse, as well as how therapy sessions help survivors and their partners deal with a history of sexual abuse. References to information obtained during this conversation are directly credited to Ms. Hoover in this text.

Chapter 11: Breaking the Cycle of Sexual Abuse

[1]   Vincent J. Felitti, M.D. "Long-term Medical Consequences of Incest, Rape, and Molestation," *Southern Medical Journal*, Vol. 84, No. 3, March 1991, p. 331.

Chapter 12: Confronting the Issue of Confrontation

[1]   Bobbi Hoover, M.A. telephone interview; see reference under Chapter 9 notes.

[2]   Kathy Duguid, M.A. telephone interview; see reference under Chapter 9 notes.

Chapter 13: A Survivor's Choices

[1] Carol Poston and Karen Lison, *Reclaiming Our Lives: Hope for Adult Survivors of Incest* (Bantam Books, 1990), 20-21.

[2] Bobbi Hoover, M.A. telephone interview; see reference under Chapter 9 notes.

Chapter 14: My Body, My Self

[1] Margaret Matthews. "Learning to Reweave the Silken Threads That Connect Body and Mind." *The Healing Woman*, Vol. 1, No. 4, August 1992, p.3. All references to this article appearing in this chapter are directly credited to Ms. Matthews.

Afterword

[1] Terrence Des Pres, *The Survivor: An Anatomy of Life in the Death Camps* (New York: Oxford University Press, 1976), 21. **Reprinted by permission of Oxford University Press.**

Reference List

There are a number of good resources available to survivors, and I encourage you to avail yourselves of whatever help they are able to provide. Through reaching outside yourselves, you will receive affirmation of your experiences and gain hope that recovery is possible. Here, I have listed only those resources referenced in the creation of this book and useful to my own journey toward healing.

BOOKS

Barbach, Lonnie Garfield. *For Yourself: The Fulfillment of Female Sexuality.* New York: Signet. 1975.

Bass, Ellen and Laura Davis. *The Courage to Heal: A Guide for Women Survivors of Child Sexual Abuse.* New York: HarperPerennial, A Division of HarperCollins Publishers. 1992.

Blume, E. Sue. *Secret Survivors: Uncovering Incest and Its Aftereffects in Women.* New York: Ballantine Books. 1991.

Capacchione, Lucia. *Recovery of Your Inner Child.* New York: Simon & Schuster. 1991.

Davis, Laura. *Allies in Healing.* New York: HarperPerennial. 1991.

Des Pres, Terrence. *The Survivor: An Anatomy of Life in the Death Camps.* New York: Oxford University Press, Inc. 1976.

Herman, Judith Lewis, M.D. *Father-Daughter Incest.* Cambridge, Massachusetts: Harvard University Press. 1981.

Herman, Judith Lewis, M.D. *Trauma and Recovery.* New York: Basic Books, A Division of HarperCollins Publishers. 1992.

Poston, Carol and Karen Lison. *Reclaiming Our Lives: Hope for Adult Survivors of Incest.* Boston: Little, Brown and Company. 1990.

JOURNAL ARTICLES

Felitti, Vincent J., M.D. "Childhood Sexual Abuse, Depression, and Family Dysfunction in Adult Obese Patients: A Case Control Study." *Southern Medical Journal,* Vol. 86, No. 7, July 1993, pp. 732-736.

Felitti, Vincent J., M.D. "Long-term Medical Consequences of Incest, Rape, and Molestation." *Southern Medical Journal,* Vol. 84, No. 3, March 1991, pp. 328-331.

Williams, Linda Meyer, Ph.D. "Adult Memories of Childhood Abuse: Preliminary Findings from a Longitudinal Study." *The Advisor,* Summer 1992. Chicago: American Professional Society on the Abuse of Children.

NEWSLETTER

The Healing Woman, The monthly newsletter for women survivors of childhood sexual abuse. Margot Silk Forrest, Editor and Publisher; P.O. Box 3038, Moss Beach, CA 94038; 415/728-0339.

NEWSLETTER ARTICLES

Mason, Barrie Ann. "Incest, Anger, and Spirituality." *The Healing Woman,* Vol. 1, No. 5, September 1992, p. 3.

Matthews, Margaret. "Learning to Reweave the Silken Threads That Connect Body and Mind." *The Healing Woman,* Vol. 1, No. 4, August 1992, p. 3.

POSITION PAPERS

(Presented as part of a panel discussion at the Annual Meeting of the American Psychiatric Association, May 26, 1993, San Francisco, California)

Briere, John, Ph.D. "Adult Memories of Childhood Trauma: Current Controversies."

Herman, Judith Lewis, M.D. "Adult Memories of Childhood Trauma: Current Controversies."

TELEPHONE INTERVIEWS

Clinician

Felitti, Vincent J., M.D., head of the Department of Preventive Medicine at Kaiser Permanente in San Diego, California, who is studying the relationship between childhood sexual abuse and chronic health problems.

Therapists

Duguid, Kathy, M.A., Licensed Marriage, Family, Child Counselor (MFCC), of Menlo Park, California, whose clinical practice includes working extensively with incest survivors.

Hoover, Bobbi, M.A., Licensed Marriage, Family, Child Counselor (MFCC), of Santa Clara, California, whose clinical practice includes working extensively with adult incest survivors as well as out-of-home molestation survivors.

Index